CONTENTS

INTRODUCTION — 4
Basic chronology of the U-boat war in the Atlantic

CONVOY NIGHT SURFACE ATTACKS — 5
The Kretschmer method, 1940–41 . The official doctrine, 1943

DECK-GUN ATTACKS — 14
The theory: rules for interception of merchant ships . The practice . The official doctrine

SOLO MISSIONS — 21
U-47 at Scapa Flow . The Mediterranean: U-81 and U-331 . North American waters, 1942 . Far Eastern waters, 1943–44

'WOLF-PACK' ATTACKS — 29
'Free hunting' . Patrol/reporting lines . Fast patrol lines . The turn of the tide

KRIEGSMARINE-LUFTWAFFE CO-OPERATION — 37
The Fw 200C Condor . Combined air-sea strikes

ASSOCIATED EQUIPMENT — 40
Bachstelze ('Wagtail') . Midget submarines

OFFENSIVE WEAPONS — 43
Torpedoes . Torpedo guidance systems . Mines

DEFENSIVE EQUIPMENT — 49
Radar decoys . Sonar decoys . Protective coatings

DEFENSIVE TACTICS — 55
Against warships . Against aircraft

SELECT BIBLIOGRAPHY — 63

INDEX — 64

U-BOAT TACTICS IN WORLD WAR II

INTRODUCTION

Grossadmiral Karl Dönitz, Commander Submarines and later C-in-C Navy, whose own younger son was lost in U-954 in May 1943. The care shown by Dönitz for his crews' welfare and the interest he took in the development of tactics stemmed from his extensive combat experience as a U-boat officer in World War I. (Deutsches U-Boot Museum)

From the small, early Type II coastal submarines, through to the handful of advanced Type XXI and Type XXIII boats that got to sea in the final months, German U-boat design and production was forced into continual development and improvement to keep pace with wartime needs. Paramount among these was the challenge of having to face increasingly effective Allied anti-submarine warfare (ASW) efforts, and – like the submarines themselves – tactics for their effective employment needed continuous analysis and adjustment.

Submarines were employed in a variety of roles, from coastal patrols, through individual opportunist actions by single unsupported U-boats – both in the Atlantic and in more distant waters – to co-ordinated 'wolf-pack' ambushes far out in the North Atlantic. Numerous tactics were developed, some more successful than others, in attempts to help submarine commanders achieve combat success, and the Oberkommando der Kriegsmarine (OKM – Navy High Command) went as far as producing a *U-Boat Commander's Handbook* to disseminate the practical lessons learned by the most successful captains.

We now know, of course – as they did not – that from around August 1941 the U-Boat Arm was hugely handicapped by the British cracking of the Kriegsmarine's 'Enigma'-encrypted radio traffic between boats at sea and the Befehlshaber der Unterseeboote (Commander, Submarines – the headquarters staff of Adm Karl Dönitz). The Bletchley Park centre needed continual radio intercepts and up-dated decryptions to supply the consequent 'Ultra' intelligence, but this often allowed the Allies to route convoys to frustrate German interception, and even to deploy assets to lie in wait at designated rendezvous between far-ranging U-boats and their resupply ships. Nevertheless, on the occasions when the Allies failed to intercept or decrypt message traffic, and the Germans applied the requisite tactics effectively, the U-boats were capable of inflicting devastating damage on Allied shipping, particularly in the vital North Atlantic sealanes upon which the war effort in the European theatre depended.

CONVOY NIGHT SURFACE ATTACKS

Such attacks were pioneered by the most successful of the 'ace' commanders, Korvettenkapitän Otto Kretschmer, who discovered early in the war that attacks on convoys were easier when made on the surface under the cover of darkness.

With the boat trimmed low in the water, the small conning tower was very difficult for any lookout on a merchantman or warship to spot. A further benefit of attacking on the surface was that the U-boat, powered by its diesel engines, could move much faster and further than it could underwater when reliant on electrical power. (For instance, the Type VII boat had a top surface speed and range of c.17 knots and 8,100 nautical miles, but the submerged figures were 7.3 knots, and only 69 miles before recharging the batteries.) Its surface speed would certainly be faster than that of the merchant convoys, and of some of the smaller escorts protecting them. Additionally, the escorts' 'Asdic' (sonar) equipment – for acoustic underwater location and ranging – could not detect a submarine running on the surface.

The U-boat would approach the convoy submerged, and, ideally, gain a position on its beam and slightly ahead. Having identified a gap in the escort screen, it would surface and 'sprint' through the perimeter screen and into the heart of the convoy formation. An ideal attack position was at right angles to the overlapping parallel columns of merchant ships, which would thus present the widest possible target area. The real prizes for the U-boats were the large oil tankers and munitions ships, which would be placed at the centre of the convoy to give them the greatest protection. This precaution was to some extent effective against attacks by submerged submarines – which would struggle to penetrate deeply into the convoy without being detected by the escorts' Asdic – but not against surface attack.

At an ideal distance of somewhere between 400m and 1,000m, torpedoes would be launched (the torpedo would not 'arm' until it had run about 300 metres). It was normal practice to launch a full salvo of torpedoes at several targets rather than selecting a single ship for attack, for the simple reason that once a torpedo had detonated and the convoy had become aware of the U-boat's presence further attacks became more difficult and dangerous.

Kapitänleutnant Kurt Diggins, commanding the Type VIIC boat U-458, is shown at the navigation or 'sky' periscope in the relatively spacious control room. This larger of the two periscopes was used predominantly for scanning the horizon and sky for enemy ships and aircraft, and also to take bearings. KL Diggins survived the sinking of his boat in August 1943, and outlived the war. (Deutsches U-Boot Museum)

The U-boat would generally launch its first torpedo, with the longest running time, against the furthest target: in theory this allowed the time to aim and fire at subsequent targets in a sequence that produced almost simultaneous strikes by all the torpedoes. (For instance, on 23/24 August 1940 KL Erich Topp's little Type IIC boat U-57 sank three freighters with a single fast salvo from its three bow tubes.)

Taking advantage of the confusion resulting from a successful attack, the U-boat would slip out of the convoy, still on the surface, while the escorts sped off to hunt what they probably thought was a submerged boat at a much greater distance. If the boat successfully evaded detection during its withdrawal, it would reload its torpedo tubes and prepare for further action. If it was detected by escorts, then – depending on the type of warship – it might try to put some distance between it and the pursuer while still motoring on the surface, building up forward momentum in order to shorten the time taken to crash-dive (normally at least 25–30 seconds). At the forefront of the commander's mind,

Basic chronology of U-boat war in Atlantic

1939 *September:* at outbreak of war, U-Bootwaffe has 57 boats, of which 23 are at sea in Western waters; but only 25 of total are Type VIIs, capable of Atlantic operations. From north German bases, they must either attempt to run the dangerous English Channel, or sail up the North Sea and round the north of Scotland before breaking out into Irish waters and the Atlantic. OKW considers the U-boat war as a secondary effort. *October:* U-47's penetration of Royal Navy's Scapa Flow fleet base demonstrates potential of independent submarine missions, bringing the Commander Submarines, Kapitän z S Karl Dönitz, promotion to flag rank. By end of year 106 Allied and neutral cargo ships have been sunk, 102 of them while sailing alone.

1940 Early in year British convoy system slowly takes shape, and torpedo failures hamper U-boat attacks. *July:* German capture of French Atlantic ports eliminates long approach voyages, greatly extending operational range and air support in Atlantic. *August:* new rules of engagement allow unrestricted blockade of Great Britain. During this 'Happy Time', c.833,740 tons of shipping are sunk in *June–August*, and in *September–November* c.784,400 tons. *November:* first (unsuccessful) British radar-assisted attack on a U-boat. Most small Type II boats withdrawn to Baltic for use by training flotillas; at end of year only 22 U-boats are at sea in Atlantic. During 1940, 54 new boats are commissioned and 26 lost; they sink c.492 cargo ships, totalling c.2.37 million tons.

1941 'Happy Time' ends in spring, as Allied ASW capabilities steadily improve; RAF aircraft equipped with ASV Mk II radar start to hunt boats on surface. *March:* US Lend-Lease Act brings Britain 50 old destroyers to increase escort strength; from *April*, British naval and air bases in Iceland, and later US bases in Greenland, slowly improve Atlantic cover, but still leave large 'air gap'. The USA effectively anticipates entry into the war by taking responsibility for convoy escorts west of Greenland, while U-boats are still forbidden to attack US ships (though some do). *May:* First improved Type 271 search radar fitted to RN warships. Boarding party from HMS *Bulldog* captures U-110 intact, complete with 'Enigma' machine and documents. *July:* first HFDF equipment installed on British warships, allowing long-range location of U-boats on surface by tracking their radio signals; by *October* its use is widespread. *December:* Germany declares war on USA. RAF base in Iceland receives No.120 Sqn with first B-24 Liberator long-range bombers. During 1941, 202 U-boats are commissioned and 38 lost; U-boats claim c.445 ships sunk, totalling c.2.1 million tons.

1942 *December 1941–July 1942:* 'Second Happy Time'; U-boats sink c.3 million tons of shipping in Atlantic for loss of 14 boats, of which only six of 21 operating in Western Atlantic – in *February* alone they sink 69 ships in US/Canadian waters. *June:* first RAF night interception of U-boat on surface using 'Leigh Light' searchlight; Coastal Command now has two squadrons with B-24 and B-17, in addition to long-range Catalina and Sunderland flying boats. Increasing Allied ASW capability forces some U-boats south to Caribbean, and South Atlantic off Brazilian and African coasts, where they achieve many successes. *September–November*, c.510,000 tons of Allied Atlantic shipping sunk. By *October*, Dönitz has 212 boats, of which c.70 at sea at any one time – but so are growing numbers of new British AS frigates and, by end of year, seven new escort aircraft carriers. *November:* Allied assets, including new 'support groups' (see below) and escort carriers, distracted southwards to support Operation 'Torch' landings in French North Africa; c.743,320 tons of Allied shipping sunk – highest ever monthly total. During 1942, 238 U-boats are commissioned and 88 lost; they sink c.1,094 cargo ships totalling c.5.8 million tons.

1943 Heavy winter storms hamper both sides. *January:* First greatly improved ASV Mk III centimetric radar sets ordered for RAF Coastal Command. Hitler, incensed at failure of Kriegsmarine surface units to cut Arctic convoy route by which the Allies support the USSR, replaces Adm Raeder at head of the OKM with Adm Dönitz, but latter remains BdU. *January–March*, c.1.19 million tons of Allied shipping lost. *March:* last very bad month for Allies. 16–20 March: greatest convoy battle, when 44 U-boats are vectored to attack 'traffic jam' of convoys HX-229 and SC-122, total 91 ships; 19 boats actually make attacks and 13 of them achieve hits, sinking 22 ships totalling c.146,600 tons, for loss of one U-boat.

Typically, only a strictly limited number of crew members were permitted on the bridge – usually just the commander or watch officer, plus enough lookouts to ensure coverage of all quarters. Orders stressed that during a surface action the lookouts must not allow themselves to become distracted by events, but were to maintain their watch over their assigned sectors at all times. (Author's collection)

However, with return of assets from 'Torch' deployments at end of March, **Allied ASW forces then decisively seize initiative**. Many more escorts and small carriers become available, and mid-Atlantic 'air gap' is finally closed by these and by long-range aircraft from USA, Canada, Iceland and UK. Deployment of separate support groups, to reinforce convoy escorts at need, allows persistent hunting-down of located U-boats while escort groups sail on with convoy. Groups are directed by both ships and planes, the latter increasingly equipped with short-wave centimetric radar, whose high definition makes it dangerous for U-boats to run on surface at night. Forced to spend most of the time submerged, running on much slower electric motors, boats have greater difficulty intercepting convoys, and are vulnerable to improved ASW weapons and tactics. From 16 U-boats lost in March and 15 in April, in May 1943 losses suddenly rise to 42 boats sunk (of c.112 at sea). 24 May, Adm Dönitz temporarily withdraws U-boats from North Atlantic.

September: Gruppe 'Leuthen' of 21 boats returns to convoy lanes, with radar-detectors, T5 acoustic torpedoes, *Aphrodite* and *Bolde* decoys; they destroy six freighters and (with the T5) four escorts, for loss of three boats. *September–October*: 21 boats of Gruppe 'Rossbach' lose six sunk and four badly damaged, for only two Allied ships sunk. *October:* 13-strong Gruppe 'Schliefen' sinks only one freighter out of 117, but loses six U-boats; Dönitz then suspends campaign once again. Many attacks are frustrated by aircraft; radar-detectors still do not pick up airborne centimetric pulses, and if they detect ships' radar it merely gives U-boats a chance to dive 'into the cellar', where they are at a disadvantage. Overall, results with acoustic torpedoes will fall well short of hopes. *September–November*: Allied monthly losses average only c.60,000 tons – less than 10 per cent of 1942 results – and during second half of year average survival expectancy for U-boats in Atlantic is calculated at 1.5 patrols. During 1943, 290 boats are commissioned but 245 lost; they sink 451 Allied cargo ships, totalling c.2.39 million tons – less than half the results for 1942.

* * *

Although the see-saw competition in technical developments continues until the end of the war – with Germany building a few very advanced submarines that would influence post-war designs, and many U-boats achieving individual successes – after May 1943 the U-Boat Arm is no longer a potentially war-winning weapon, and becomes a wasting asset. The Allied navies become ever stronger, better equipped and more tactically practised, and the strategic bombing campaign on Germany hampers the boat-building programme. Catastrophic personnel losses also mean that the boats that do get to sea are crewed by hastily trained men led by inexperienced officers. Germany never catches up with the Allies' lead in the ASW applications of radar; most of the older and more successful U-boat commanders are dead; and co-ordinated 'wolf packs' quickly become a thing of the past.

In *January–March 1944*, c.3,360 Allied cargo ships cross the Atlantic in 105 convoys; only three ships are sunk by U-boats, but 36 boats are lost. In *January–June* between 20 and 30 per cent of all U-boats on patrol are lost every month, and many others abort their missions due to heavy damage from aircraft attacks. The loss of the French Atlantic ports in *June–August 1944* essentially ends the U-boat war. During 1944 the 230 boats commissioned are exceeded by 264 lost, and surviving units are limited to bases in remote Norway or bomb-ravaged northern Germany. In 1944 they sink only 131 Allied ships, totalling c.702,000 tons. In *January–April 1945*, 92 boats are commissioned but 139 lost; on Germany's capitulation in early May there are still about 50 U-boats at sea, but most captains have long been preoccupied with mere survival.

More than 1,100 U-boats were commissioned between June 1935 and May 1945, of which some 920 sailed on war patrols; about 800 of these were sunk, in roughly equal proportions by Allied warships and aircraft. Nevertheless, although about three-quarters of the total fleet never even damaged a single Allied ship, the contribution of some 320 of the boats to Germany's war effort had been remarkable. They had sunk about 2,840 of the roughly 5,150 Allied and neutral merchantmen lost in all seas, totalling c.14.3 million tons (compared with some 800 ships sunk by German aircraft, and 540 by mines).

During surface torpedo attacks the firing orders were issued by the First Watch Officer (IWO) from the bridge, using the UZO (U-Boot Zieloptik) equipment – heavy-duty binoculars attached to a pedestal mount. These connected directly to the torpedo aiming system, an electro-mechanical calculator in the commander's attack position in the conning tower. (Deutsches U-Boot Museum)

however, would be the knowledge that if the warship scored a hit on the submarine with its main armament then damage to the pressure hull might render it incapable of diving, in which case it was certainly doomed.

The Kretschmer method, 1940–41

In April 1940 Otto Kretschmer, already a seasoned and successful veteran of eight war patrols, took command of a new Type VIIB boat, the U-99. During a night training exercise in fairly rough seas Kretschmer was stalking a 'convoy' when, seeing that the moon was about to disappear behind heavy cloud cover, he amazed his crew by telling them they would intercept on the surface. Kretschmer coolly slipped past the escorts, achieved a perfect attack position, then switched on his searchlight to indicate a hit; the defenders were forced to admit defeat.

Training over, U-99 began its short but very successful combat career. On 1 August 1940, Kretschmer spotted convoy OB-191 and decided to put his preferred tactic into operation. Stalking the convoy by day to achieve a perfect attack position, he was delighted to see the escorts speed off to the north, presumably to hunt another suspected U-boat, and as darkness fell he surfaced and slipped into the convoy. Early on 2 August, at a range of 600m, he fired a torpedo that hit the 10,970-ton tanker *Strinda*. His second shot, from a distance of just 500m, hit a second tanker, the 6,550-ton *Lucerna*. Kretschmer then launched a torpedo at a large merchant ship; this missed the intended target but passed her to strike amidships yet another tanker, the 8,000-ton *Alexia*. As the convoy scattered, U-99, trimmed low in the water and still undetected, was in some danger of being unintentionally rammed by one of the merchantmen, but in fact Kretschmer was rewarded by seeing two ships that were manoeuvring to avoid the unseen U-boat collide with each other.

The *Alexia*, though damaged, was still afloat, and since the escorts were still absent Kretschmer took the opportunity to man his 8.8cm deck gun and speed up the sinking of the tanker by sending about 30 rounds into her hull. During this action one of his lookouts spotted the searchlight of an approaching escort, but even then Kretschmer decided not to dive, withdrawing into the darkness on the surface. He had triumphantly validated his theories, and was well on the way to achieving his goal of 'one torpedo, one ship'.

On 21 September 1940, U-99 took part in an attack on convoy HX-72, once again slipping into the convoy on the surface. Kretschmer's first shot hit the 9,150-ton tanker *Invershannon*, which slowly began to settle. His next victim was the 3,660-ton freighter *Baron Blythswood*, which took a torpedo from a range of around 800m and sank within 40 seconds. Through the gap this left in the convoy, Kretschmer spotted another target; the 5,150-ton freighter *Elmbank* was the next to be torpedoed. Meanwhile the escorts, assuming a conventional submerged attack, were busy racing around the perimeter of the convoy searching for an underwater enemy. Kretschmer remained on the surface while the convoy passed his boat, making no attempt to dive or to retreat.

The *Elmbank*, carrying a cargo of timber, was not yet sinking, and neither a second torpedo nor several shells from U-99's deck gun succeeded in finishing her off. Incredibly, Kretschmer then took the time to reload his tubes with the spare torpedoes stored outside the pressure hull under the decking – a lengthy and complex process, during which it would have been impossible to dive should any escort vessel appear. Kretschmer then fired a second torpedo at the *Invershannon*, which was also sinking too slowly for his liking, and this sent her to the bottom. He next turned his attention back to the *Elmbank*, just as a second U-boat appeared – KK Günther Prien's U-47, which had also been involved in the attacks on HX-72. Both U-boats poured shells into the freighter until U-47 ran out of ammunition and departed; a few incendiaries from U-99 finally sank the *Elmbank*.

Kretschmer had once again spent the entire action on the surface, despite the presence of Allied escorts, even taking time to reload from his external torpedo stowage – yet not once was his boat spotted. He subsequently penned a lengthy report giving his recommendations for U-boat tactics, the main points of which may be summarized as follows:

Korvettenkapitän Otto Kretschmer, commander of U-99, was Germany's leading World War II U-boat 'ace' in terms of tonnage sunk (263,682 tons), despite his operational career ending in March 1941. This greatest exponent of night torpedo attacks on the surface was known as 'Silent Otto' – not for his demeanour, but because of his extreme reluctance to use his radio lest this allowed his boat to be detected and tracked by British warships. This suspicion was not universally shared; the Kriegsmarine never discovered the effectiveness of Allied radio interception and direction-finding, and wrongly supected that inexplicable encounters were due to some kind of emission from the primitive radar-detection apparatus that U-boats were issued from 1942. (Author's collection)

1. Efficient lookouts are of prime importance.
2. It is essential not simply to spot the target, but to spot it in good time.
3. Lone ships should be attacked on the surface with gunfire in order to save expensive torpedoes.
4. Survivors should be assisted where possible.
5. Convoys should only be attacked in daylight if it is not feasible to wait for nightfall.
6. Attack at night from the dark side of the convoy, so that the target is silhouetted and the submarine is in shadow.
7. When there is little or no moonlight, attack from the windward side [to avoid a visible white bow-wave when motoring into the wind].
8. Fire one torpedo per target, not fanned salvoes.
9. Fire at close range.
10. Once the attack is launched, do not submerge except in circumstances of dire necessity. Remember that on the surface it is easier for you to spot the enemy than for the enemy to spot you.
11. Dive only for two hours before dawn each day, to rest the crew, sweep with the sound detection equipment, etc.; otherwise, remain on the surface.

With regard to Point 8, the *U-Boat Commander's Handbook* does actually recommend the use of fanned shots in certain circumstances, including when the target was particularly valuable (e.g. an Allied battleship or aircraft carrier), or when several vessels were 'overlapped' or in close column astern across the field of aim. Here, a fanned salvo at relatively short range, where targeting data was reliable, should result in more than one torpedo striking the target, thus ensuring its destruction. It was also accepted that in some circumstances fanned salvos at targets from ranges of over *c.*1,000m should result in at least one hit, this being preferable to several misses with individual shots. However, a commander always had to bear in mind his modest supply of torpedoes (at this date, a maximum of 14).

Kretschmer subsequently took part in attacks on convoy SC-7 on 18/19 October 1940, when U-99 sank six ships and damaged another,

A — OPTIMUM APPROACHES FOR SURFACED U-BOAT EARLY IN WAR

(Obviously, these presentations are not to scale.)

1: Daytime
This shows the approach of a U-boat towards a small unescorted convoy. Early on a bright morning, the boat is approaching from the east; by closing with the convoy while trimmed low in the water, bows-on and out of the sun, the commander makes the small forward aspect as hard as possible for lookouts to spot. On this occasion he also has the advantage of approaching from up-wind, which prevents his boat throwing a visible bow-wave of spray. Once the convoy's range, course and formation are established he will almost certainly submerge to work his way round into an ideal attack position, from a flank.

2: Night-time
The U-boat is making its general approach facing towards the moon, from behind and up-wind of the convoy; its surface speed of *c.*15 knots allows it to catch up with a slow convoy sailing at about 8 knots. The merchant ships are highlighted against the moon and the horizon, while the relatively tiny profile of the surfaced submarine is almost invisible in the darkness. It cannot be detected by the escort warships' Asdic, and – prior to the general installation of efficient search radar on escorts – would be almost undetectable. The direction of the moonlight improves the U-boat bridge watch's chances of spotting any roving escort (see flanks of convoy) before it gets dangerously close.

Two views of a U-boat engine room, showing the two banks of MAN diesel engines (2800–3200hp in Type VII boats, 4400hp in Type IX) that propelled the boat on the surface, and which charged the batteries for the electric motors (Type VII, 750hp; Type IX, 1000hp) for submerged running.

totalling around 30,500 tons; and on 16 March 1941, during attacks on HX-112, he sank six ships totalling 43,100 tons. The tremendous results Kretschmer achieved by night surface attacks led to the wider use of this tactic, though no other commander ever rivalled his outstanding success. He had nevertheless proved that those with the steely nerves required to sneak into the middle of a convoy on the surface under the cover of darkness, and to calmly attack individual targets with single torpedoes rather than taking the easy option of firing a spread of four, could achieve remarkable results.

Ironically, given his preference for remaining on the surface, during his last convoy attack on 17 March 1941 Kretschmer was below decks when his watch officer ordered the boat to dive. It was immediately detected by the destroyer HMS *Walker* and subjected to a heavy depth-charge attack, which forced the damaged U-99 to the surface. Kretschmer ordered his crew to abandon ship, and he and the majority of his men were rescued, to spend the rest of the war in a PoW camp.

The official doctrine, 1943

The 1943 edition of the *U-Boat Commander's Handbook* gives the following advice regarding night surface attacks:

'In areas where contact with the enemy might be expected at night, at least one torpedo must be carried in the tube, with the tube opened and ready for action.

In the photo above, the left-hand man is an *Obermaschinist*, a technical senior petty officer, and the other the *Leitender Ingineur*, the boat's engineering officer. Since boats operated for weeks or months far from any dockyard and carried only limited spare parts, the engineering crew had to be expert and ingenious, and a close watch always had to be maintained over what appears to the layman to be a bewildering maze of dials, valves and controls. Engineering petty officers and ratings represented some two-thirds of a typical crew of about 52 all ranks. (Deutsches U-Boot Museum, and author's collection)

'Success is dependent on good eyesight. He who sees first has the advantage, so those with the best eyesight should be up on the bridge [conning tower] during a night attack. In heavy seas, wet spray can make binoculars difficult to use, so a man should be stationed in the conning tower with dry binoculars for the lookouts, and ready to wipe clean their wet binoculars.

'When a target is spotted, make top speed to attain a position ahead of the beam.

'Attack from the most favourable quarter (from the windward side, against a dark horizon, etc.) During an attack, always keep the submarine under way, never stop.

'If detected, always attempt to evade the enemy while remaining on the surface.

'After hitting the first target, go for a second and third immediately, as this will be made easier by the confusion after the detonation of the first torpedo.

'After the attack, remain on the surface to observe the results; only dive in case of dire emergency... Turn sharply towards the rear of the convoy, where the danger of being spotted and rammed is lowest.

'If able to stay on the surface, withdraw for a short distance and reload tubes. If forced to dive, do so at top speed and proceed in a straight line away from the enemy. The noise caused by torpedo hits will make it almost impossible for enemy Asdic to track the submarine.'

DECK-GUN ATTACKS

In the first year of the war the Kriegsmarine suffered severely from the unreliability of the detonators fitted to its G7 torpedoes (see below, under 'Offensive Weapons'). For example, during the Norwegian campaign of spring 1940 more than 30 out of 42 attacks on Allied warships failed due to faulty torpedoes, and although officers were sometimes blamed for imagined incompetence, several crews actually heard torpedoes striking the targets' hulls but failing to detonate. Not only were potential targets lost, but a great deal of money was wasted on highly expensive but faulty ordnance. Even if a boat was loaded with perfectly functioning torpedoes, the relatively small size of most German submarines meant that only a very limited supply of these could be carried. It was generally considered sensible to keep these for particularly valuable targets such as tankers, and when possible the 8.8cm or 10.5cm deck gun was used to despatch any smaller target found travelling alone in waters where a surfaced U-boat was unlikely to be intercepted by Allied warships or aircraft. In World War I several of the leading U-boat 'aces' had scored considerable successes with their deck guns, and although less use was made of them in World War II a good number of merchantmen fell victim to shellfire. Another benefit of surface gun attacks was that after a few shots to discourage him the merchant captain might elect simply to surrender.

Deck-gun attacks were of two basic categories: those carried out entirely by gunfire, and those when gunfire was used to deliver the *coup de grace* to a ship already crippled by a torpedo hit. The first type of action took place predominantly during the early part of the war; in fact, during September 1939 around 25 per cent of ships sunk by U-boats were

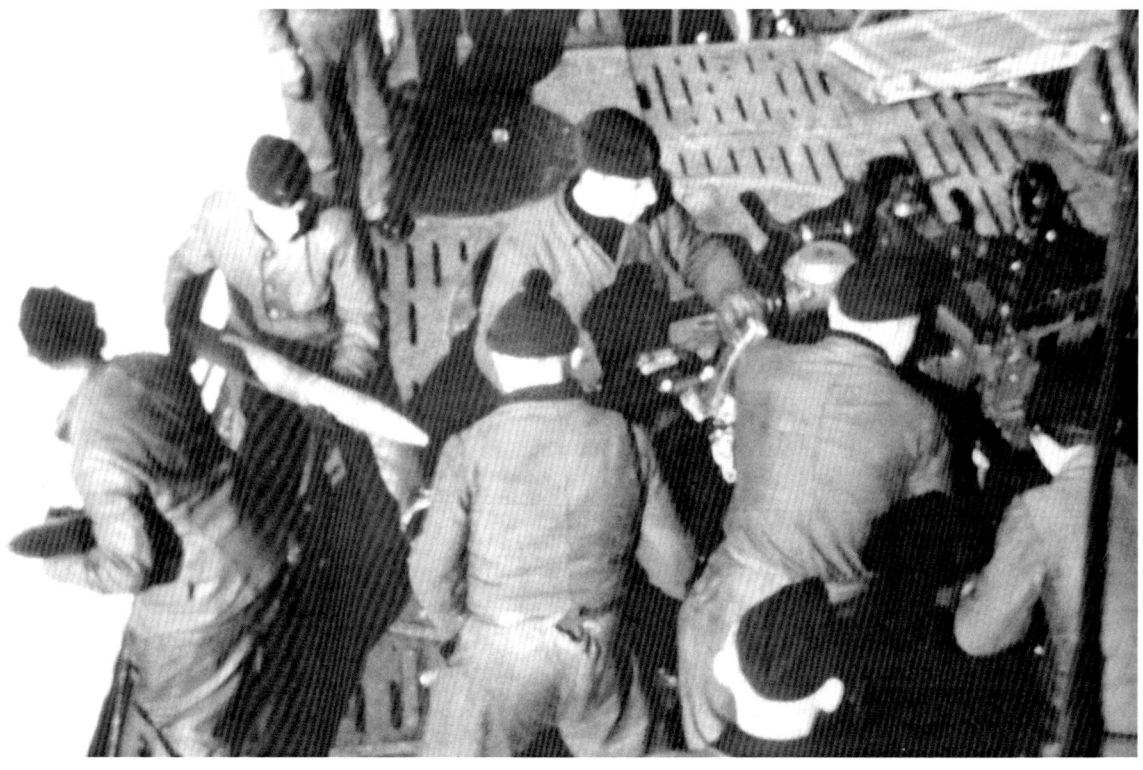

This photo was taken during gunnery training while the Type VII boat was in port; note that the seamen do not wear lifelines. Looking down from the bridge – the viewpoint of the watch officer on duty, who directed gunnery – this view shows just how little deck space was available to the gun crew; the loader and ammunition-handler at left are standing almost at the very edge of the wooden decking. The actual firing crew were the gun-layer, gunner and loader; a watertight container of 'ready' ammunition on deck close to the gun provided enough rounds for the initial engagement, after which a long, awkward chain of other crewmen had to bring up ammunition from below decks, as apparently shown here. (Deutsches U-Boot Museum)

destroyed by gunfire rather than torpedo. This statistic went some way towards persuading the Allies to install defensive guns on their merchant ships. These weapons, not always manned by well-trained crews, were not hugely effective, though any hit by an artillery shell on a U-boat could inflict potentially disabling damage.

The theory: rules for interception of merchant ships

Fundamentally, all merchant ships were to be considered suspect, and when intercepting a lone merchantman U-boat commanders were urged to exercise caution lest the apparently harmless target carried hidden guns. (The Germans had learned a hard lesson during World War I from the British use of so-called 'Q-ships' – innocent-looking steamers converted to act as decoys, luring submarines within range of their concealed weapons.)

Lone ships were to be approached submerged, and inspected from as close as possible to identify the vessel, and to detect any suspicious structures that might conceal hidden guns. At least two torpedoes were to be made ready for immediate firing. The U-boat should then surface no closer than 4,000m astern of the merchantman and order it to stop. The U-boat commander was to have clarified for himself in advance all the provisions of prize restrictions.[1]

This view towards the stern of a Type IX boat gives a good impression of its greater deck width compared with the Type VII; it was also c.21m longer, with a surfaced displacement of c.1,616 tons compared with the c.770 tons of a Type VII. The added 'comfort' of serving on a Type IX came at a cost, however: it was less manoeuvrable, and had a slower dive time – 45 seconds to reach a depth of around 20m, as opposed to 35 seconds for a Type VII. These figures assume a crash-dive when travelling at speed; from a stationary start both types took more than a minute to achieve that depth, which could be a fatal delay for a boat surprised by an aircraft. (Deutsches U-Boot Museum)

[1] The 1936 Prize Ordinance Regulations in force at the outbreak of war were both restrictive, and expressed in impenetrable bureaucratic language. Only vessels escorted by Allied warships or aircraft could be attacked without warning; otherwise the submarine commander was responsible for ensuring the safety of any merchant crew before attacking, even if the merchantman was visibly armed. In February 1940 OKM gave permission for unrestricted warfare off Britain's east and west coasts; in May 1940, in the Bay of Biscay; but only in August 1940 further out in the Atlantic.

Many Type IX boats carried a 3.7cm Flak gun on the after deck, as well as the 10.5cm main gun on the forward deck and lighter AA weapons on the 'Wintergarten' platform. Again, the extra working space for the gun crew is evident. (Deutsches U-Boot Museum)

Any resistance or refusal to obey orders to heave-to was to be dealt with ruthlessly. No members of the submarine crew should board the target, but the ship's papers were to be brought over in one of the ship's boats. At all times the submarine was to maintain its position astern of the merchantman, pointing directly towards it and thus offering the smallest potential target. An especially reliable watch-keeper should be designated to monitor the target's movements, altering the U-boat's course to maintain its relative position if necessary. The submarine should always be ready to make an emergency dive, and therefore should have no superfluous crew members on deck.

If it was decided that the vessel was carrying a war cargo and was to be sunk, the U-boat should submerge and sink it with a single torpedo from short range. If explosive charges were used instead, then a boarding party should set these at least a metre below the waterline in large compartments such as the hold and engineroom where there was space for large volumes of water to enter; portholes were to be smashed to allow air to escape as the water entered.

The practice
Otto Kretschmer, while famed for his nighttime surface torpedo attacks, also used gunfire in some actions. On one occasion, on the evening of 11 July 1940, U-99 spotted the small freighter *Merisaar* travelling alone; after one torpedo missed its target Kretschmer surfaced and, unwilling to waste any more valuable 'eels', fired a warning shot across her bows from

about 200 metres. To his surprise, the crew immediately began abandoning ship; he ordered them to return and to sail for German-occupied Bordeaux as a prize, bluffing the crew into believing that he would shadow them all the way and sink them if they attempted to escape. Sadly, the *Merisaar* was bombed and sunk by a Luftwaffe aircraft unaware that she had been captured; this robbed Kretschmer of entering the record books as the only U-boat commander to take an enemy merchant ship intact as a prize of war.

On 1 September 1940, U-99 intercepted the small steamer *Luimneach* travelling alone. Once again, a vessel of less than 1,000 tons did not warrant the expense of a torpedo, so Kretschmer surfaced and fired the usual warning shot. The crew sent a distress signal and immediately abandoned ship. Kretschmer approached to within about 100m and shelled the *Luimneach* with around 20 armour-piercing rounds and a few incendiaries, soon sending her to the bottom. Known for his humanity, he ensured that the survivors – two of whom were injured – were well provided with dressings and supplies before he left the scene.

Kretschmer was not the only one of the great 'aces' to use gunfire where appropriate. On 27 June 1940, Günther Prien's U-47 intercepted the small 2,500- ton tanker *Leticia* west of Ireland, and gunfire from 300m brought her to a halt. After the crew had abandoned ship Prien recommenced the shelling, only to see three more crew members who had hidden on board jump into the sea as the *Leticia* sank. Prien had them picked up to join their shipmates in the lifeboats; he provided the survivors with dry clothing, food and some wine before departing the scene, and they were picked up later that same day. (This was only one of several documented early-war instances of a U-boat commander going to sometimes remarkable lengths to ensure the safety of merchant crews. For example, on 7 September 1939, KL Hans-Wilhelm von Dresky of U-33 towed survivors from the SS *Olivegrove* for several hours to get them closer to land, and fired flares to attract a passing neutral ship.)

After a merchant vessel had been forced to stop by gunfire, it might be sunk either by shelling or by a close-range torpedo. This dramatic shot, taken from the bridge of the U-boat to which it fell victim, shows a torpedoed merchantman settling slowly by the stern. The *U-Boat Commander's Handbook* recommended that 'Once resistance is subdued, concentrate fire on either the bow or stern area of the target, as ships will sink faster if going down by the bow or stern than if sinking on an even keel'. The fact that this U-boat is hanging around to take photos suggests that its victim was sailing alone, and the sea and sky were clear of any Allied activity. (Author's collection)

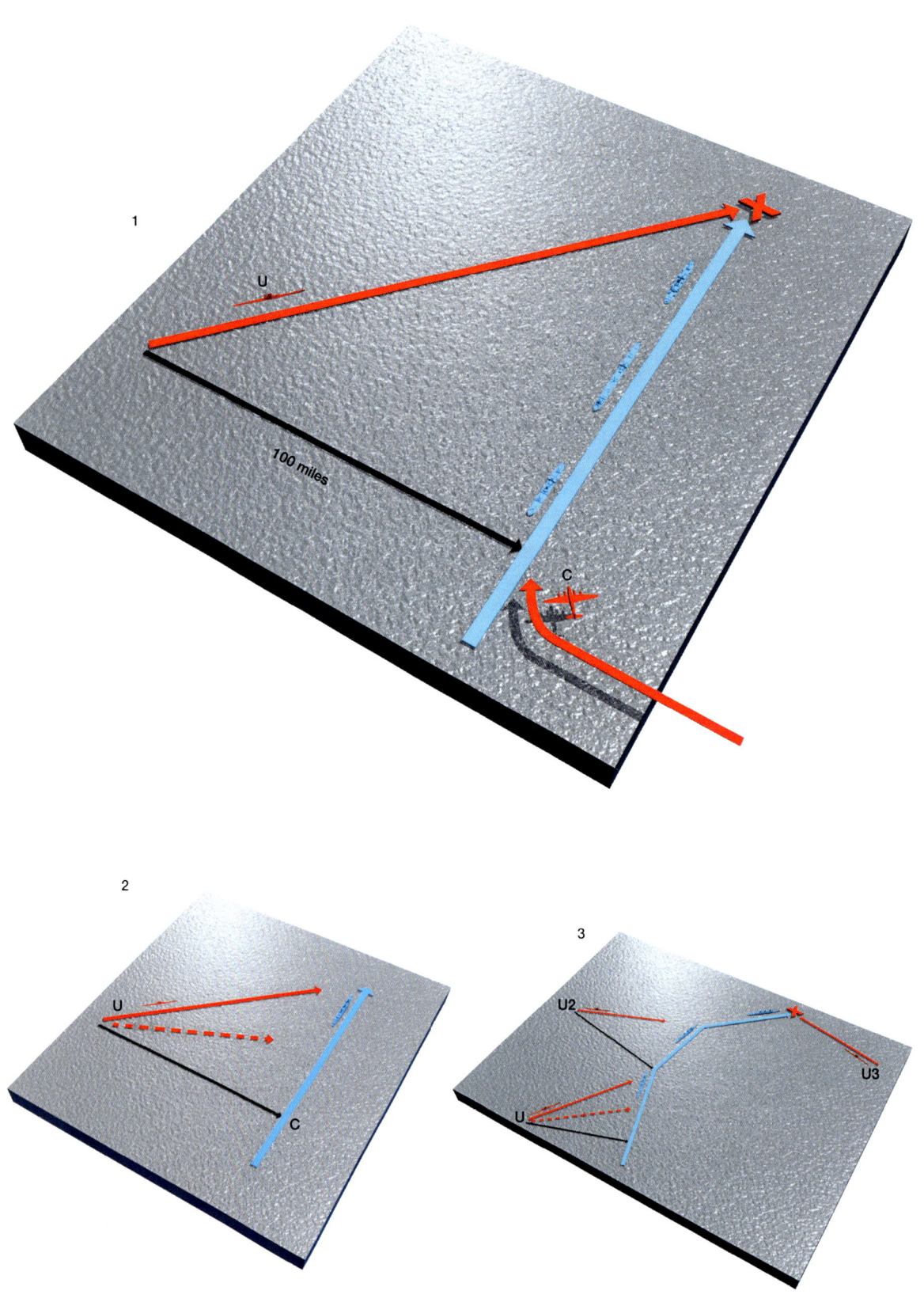

If the purpose of shelling smaller ships was to save torpedoes, however, it was often done at a considerable cost in 8.8cm ammunition. When, on 24 June 1940, Prien intercepted the small steamer *Catherine*, he brought her to a halt with a warning shot from the deck gun after two torpedoes had missed their target. The subsequent bombardment took no fewer than 113 rounds to sink the freighter, the heavy seas no doubt contributing to the difficulties faced by the gun crew. (Once again, Prien provided the survivors with rations, and they were picked up safely.)

Occasionally the deck gun would be used to force an unescorted merchantman to halt before the sitting target was despatched with a torpedo. An example of this occurred on 27 May 1943 when the Type IXD-2 boat U-181 (KK Wolfgang Lüth) intercepted the 1,600-ton *Sicilia* and stopped her with a few shells. Lüth ordered the crew to abandon ship, and then moved to an ideal torpedo attack position to send her to the bottom.

While most of the examples quoted were small vessels of under 2,000 tons' displacement, larger ships were occasionally tackled with gunfire. On 30 November 1942, Lüth's U-181 had missed the 4,150-ton *Cleanthis* with two torpedoes. U-181 was one of the so-called 'monsoon boats' that operated in the South Atlantic and on into the Indian Ocean. (Thirty of these large ocean-going Type IXD-2 submarines were built; very capacious and with a range of up to 32,000 miles, they were too unwieldy for convoy battles in the North Atlantic. With their war patrols sometimes lasting longer than 200 days, resupply was problematic for the 'monsoon boats', and torpedoes had to be carefully husbanded.) Lüth surfaced and opened fire with his 10.5cm deck gun, a much more powerful weapon than the 8.8cm carried by the Type VII boats. Most of the roughly 80 shells fired hit their target, but it was about 90 minutes before the *Cleanthis* sank, even though the boat's 3.7cm and 2cm Flak cannon joined in the bombardment. (Unfortunately for U-181's crew, the use of gunfire was not always without incident; when Lüth used all his guns to finish off the 5,980-ton *Empire Whimbrel* after first torpedoing her on 11 April 1943, a gunbarrel exploded at the first shot, mortally wounding one of the gun crew.)

B **CONVOY INTERCEPTION BY SINGLE U-BOATS**

1: The main diagram shows the optimum position for a U-boat – **(U)** – patrolling alone in 1940–41. A Condor patrol-bomber has spotted a convoy at point **(C)**, some 100 nautical miles from the position of the U-boat, and has estimated its speed at approximately 8 knots, classifying this as a 'slow convoy'. The convoy's heading is being reported to the Luftwaffe's Marine Gruppe West command at Lorient, and thence to BdU nearby. Once alerted by BdU, the U-boat commander will plot an interception course, confident that his boat's surface speed will allow him to gain a suitable attack position ahead of the convoy, at point **(X)**.

2: This represents the same scenario but where the target is a 'fast convoy', with a top speed of at least 14 knots; this was often the case with, for example, troopships, several of which were former passenger liners capable of impressive speeds. Here neither the U-boat's original course (broken line), nor a new and more north-easterly course adopted after receiving radio intelligence (solid line) can enable the submarine to intercept the convoy in time.

3: In this scenario, a second U-boat further north-east at position **(U2)** would also be unable to catch up with the fast-moving convoy, which may be warned by Allied radio-intercept intelligence to alter course. Only a third boat, fortuitously patrolling ahead of the convoy's course at position **(U3)**, would have any chance of attaining a suitable attack position. If any circumstance of visibility, sea state, escort action or a failed initial torpedo launch frustrated its flank attack, this boat too would probably be unable to pursue fast enough to try again.

Dönitz's greatest problem was that he never had enough boats at sea to ensure really effective coverage of the vast North Atlantic battlefield. These scenarios also emphasize the absolute importance of U-boats being able to travel safely on the surface; their top submerged speed of about 7 knots was completely inadequate for manoeuvring against a fast target.

Under the rules of engagement in force at the outbreak of war, after halting a merchant ship the U-boat commander was supposed to order it to send a boat across with the ship's papers detailing its cargo and destination. Automatic weapons such as MG 34s and machine pistols were to be brought up to the submarine's bridge to cover the boat as it approached, in case its occupants made any attempt to attack the submarine crew, e.g. by throwing grenades. This photo from much later in the war, showing the upper Flak platform of an up-armed Type VIIC boat with two twin 2cm AA guns, is interesting in also showing (left) two twin 7.92mm machine guns. (Deutsches U-Boot Museum)

Weather and sea state were naturally a limitation on such tactics, since the narrow deck of a submarine provided a very poor gun platform in anything but a dead calm – even a moderate swell resulted in the boat pitching and rolling. Gun crews were secured by lifelines (which were also used by bridge crews in rough seas) to prevent them being washed overboard. Given that many merchantmen carried at least some form of defensive armament, during the cautious approach they would be covered not only by the main deck and anti-aircraft guns but by machine guns brought up to the bridge from below. Particular target areas would obviously be any visible gun mounts, and also the bridge, which would be attacked with incendiary shells in order to prevent the radio room from sending out distress signals that would betray the U-boat's location. Once the target had been rendered helpless the deck-gun crew could fire at will around its waterline, but the expenditure of shells required to sink a ship might be considerable, depending on its size and the nature of its sometimes buoyant cargo.

As during surface torpedo attacks, the bridge crew had to concentrate strictly on keeping an all-round watch. To be caught unawares during a gun attack was particularly dangerous, since extra time had to be taken to stow the gun and recover its crew and the members of the ammunition chain before the boat could dive.

The official doctrine

The *U-Boat Commander's Handbook* makes it clear that boats were to use gunnery 'only for the purpose of stopping steamers, or of overcoming the resistance of unarmed or weakly armed vessels'. Its instructions may be summarized as follows:

'Before surfacing, the gun crew should assemble in the control room ready for action, and with all necessary equipment, in order to get the gun into action in the fastest possible time [after surfacing].

'The gun commander and crew must take up their positions in good time (especially for night attacks, to allow the crew's eyesight to adjust to the darkness)... The order "Ready to Fire" should not be given until the gun commander [watch officer], from his vantage point up in the conning tower, has satisfied himself that all conditions are favourable... Ammunition must be protected from becoming wet, as wet ammunition can cause the shell case to burst.

'The bombardment will commence with ten incendiary shells fired at the bridge area of the target. The fires from the incendiary shells will provide a good aiming point for subsequent shelling. The 3.7cm Flak gun is to be used to suppress the stern gun on the enemy ship, if carried, and the light 2cm Flak is only to be used on the commander's orders, if the 3.7cm gun jams.

'After identifying the armament, if any, carried by the enemy, the submarine should ideally approach from astern of the target, opening fire as soon as it is level with the target. The target should be hit no later than with the second shot [i.e. ideally only one ranging shot should be needed]. Fire should be concentrated on one area of the target, not spread around.

'If enemy resistance continues after the initial bombardment, concentrate fire from the main armament and 3.7cm Flak on the enemy gun, firing [the latter] in bursts of 6 to 8 rounds... Once the bombardment is seen to be having the desired effect, the submarine should move to the opposite side of the target in order to keep watch [i.e. to avoid the approach of an Allied ship being hidden by the target]... If the enemy gunnery is accurate and quickly finds the range of the submarine, the submarine must turn away or submerge rather than risk damage.'

* * *

As the war dragged on, and Allied ASW measures became ever more effective, opportunities for U-boats to use their deck guns safely all but disappeared, and few commanders would consider taking the risk of surfacing for such an action. Deck guns were omitted during the construction of new boats, and the majority of Type VII boats had their 8.8cm guns removed from mid-1943, since they had become little more than unnecessary weight and drag while serving no useful purpose. Nevertheless, some of the ocean-going Type IXD-2 boats still retained the 10.5cm gun; it remained a potentially useful weapon for those operating in distant waters, where ships sailing alone might still be intercepted without the degree of danger presented by Allied warships and aircraft in the Atlantic.

SOLO MISSIONS

The types of mission for which only a single U-boat would be deployed fell into a number of categories, of which the most significant were as follows:

Einzelstellung A single boat operating within a defined patrol area. The boat would regularly report weather conditions and any detected

Kapitänleutnant Günther Prien is seen here on the bridge of U-47, some time after his successful penetration of the Royal Navy fleet anchorage at Scapa Flow and sinking of HMS *Royal Oak* on 14/15 October 1939. Prien earned the nickname of 'the Bull of Scapa Flow', and one of his crew painted a cartoon of a snorting bull on the side of the conning tower; this eventually became the emblem not only of Prien's boat, but of the whole 7. U-Flotille based at St Nazaire. (Deutsches U-Boot Museum)

shipping movements back to operational control, and would not attack unless ordered to do so.

Freijagd A single boat operating in a designated patrol area, where the commander would have the discretion to attack as necessary.

Lauerstellung A single boat despatched to an area through which shipping was expected to pass, where it would literally 'lie in wait' hoping to intercept targets.

Other special solo missions might involve anything from landing agents, or laying mines around an enemy harbour, to attacks like that of U-47 on the Royal Navy fleet base at Scapa Flow.

During the early months of the war the British had not yet fully adopted the convoy system and the majority of shipping sailed independently, so for several of Germany's small U-boat fleet to have been concentrated in patrol lines in order to intercept individual ships would have been nonsensical.

C CONVOY FORMATIONS

1: Early war

Only a limited number of British and Canadian escorts are available to protect this convoy of merchantmen (**M**) in the first years of the war. Two destroyers (**D**) guard the forward quarters, with two smaller corvettes (**C**) guarding the port and starboard flanks, and two more bringing up the rear. With a considerable area of sea to guard, theses escorts would spend much of their time racing around their sectors of responsibility like sheepdogs. These necessary manoeuvres would leave considerable gaps through which a skilled U-boat commander would be able to pass, especially if brave enough to make the attempt on the surface under cover of darkness. (Constant manoeuvring, and heavy winter seas, burned up the escorts' fuel, sometimes forcing them to withdraw altogether if the sea state prevented them refuelling from an accompanying tanker.)

2: Late war

Attacking this larger and more heavily protected convoy in c.1943 would be a much more hazardous operation, even if a sizeable 'wolf pack' had been assembled. A screen of destroyers (**D**) lead the merchantmen, with others on the flanks and rear quarters. Filling the gaps between the destroyers are a number of corvettes (**C**). Bringing up the rear are smaller warships, either minesweepers or armed trawlers (**AT**); as well as providing rear cover, these would pick up survivors of any sunken ships while the more powerful escorts continued with the convoy. Within the body of the convoy is a small escort aircraft carrier (**AC**) to provide air cover. Any particularly valuable cargo vessels, such as munitions ships and oil tankers (**T**), would also be positioned in the relative safety of the centre of the convoy.

1

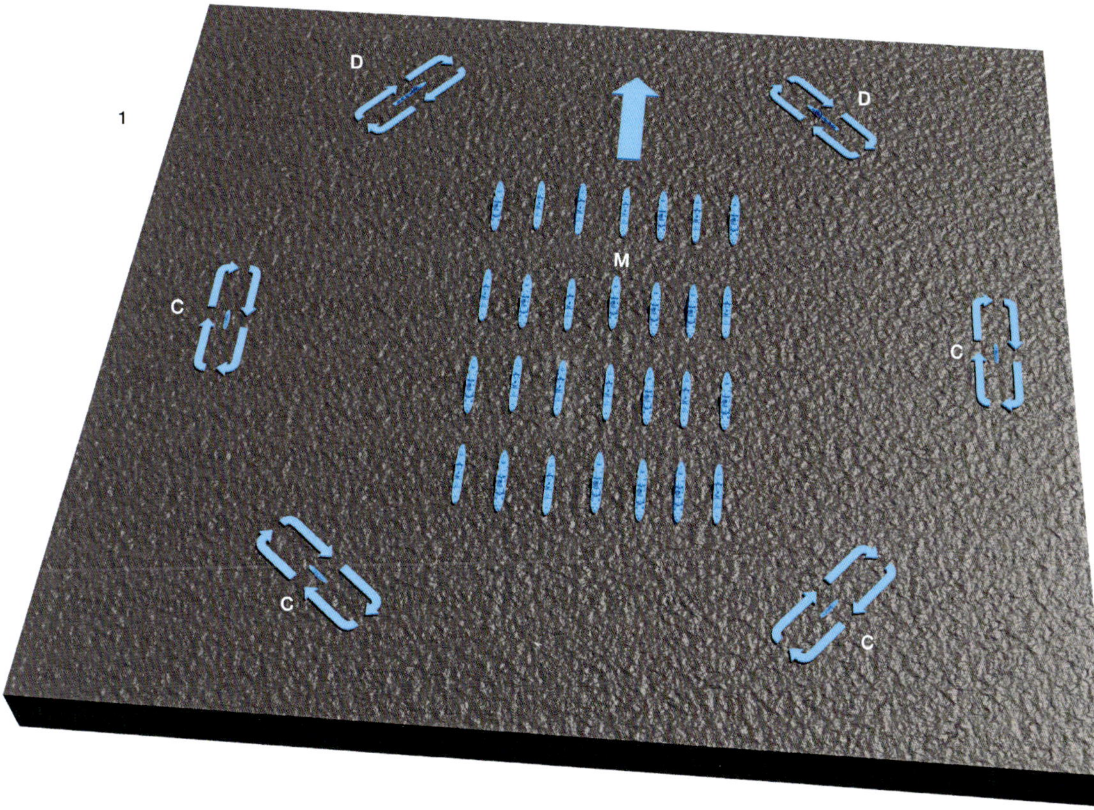

2

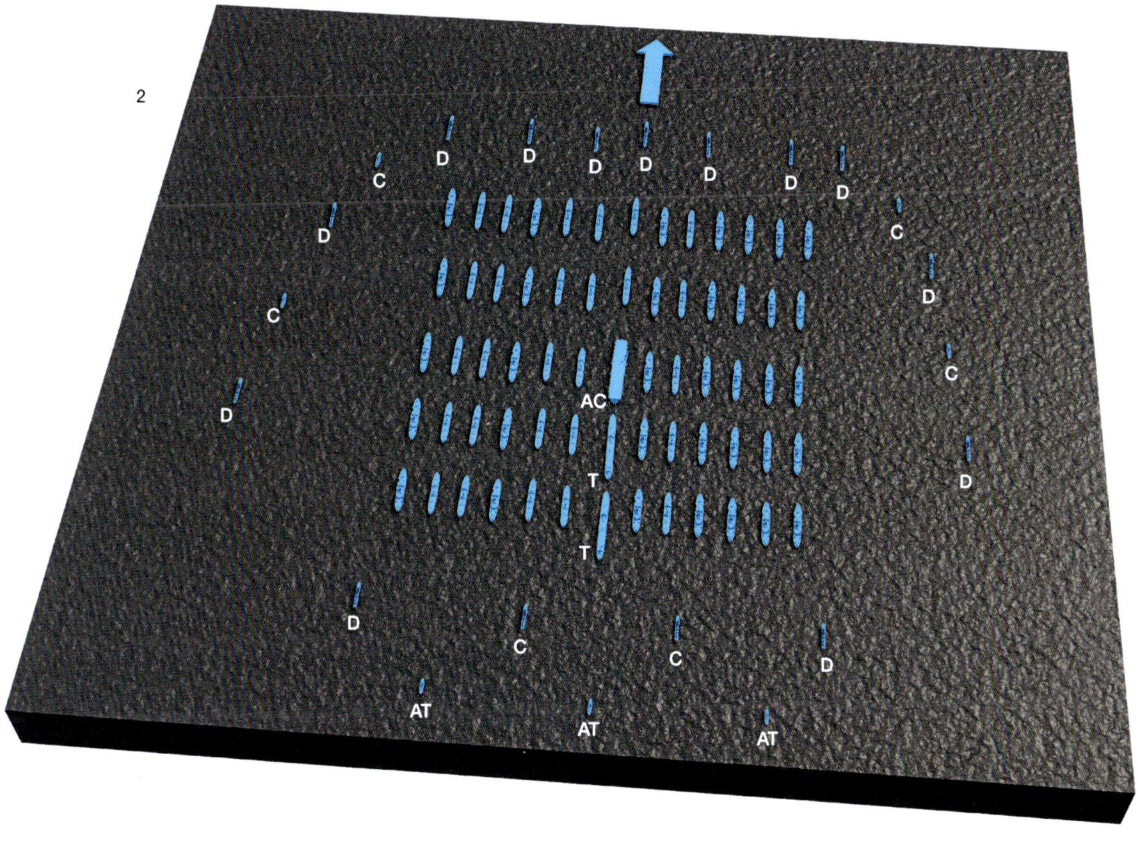

KL Prien's daring attack at Scapa Flow proved that well-planned solo missions against specific targets were a valid tactic, at least in the early part of the war. They were less feasible from 1942/43 onwards, when the pool of expert seamanship offered by the older, pre-war captains had been removed by death or by promotion to senior commands ashore. The 32 most successful 'ace' commanders – about 2 per cent of the total – accounted for nearly 30 per cent of Allied shipping losses in the Atlantic; on average, these officers were aged about 28 at the outbreak of war, and had already served in the Navy for nearly ten years. In wartime, especially after 1942, training inevitably became hastier and the introduction to combat more challenging. In the Atlantic and North Sea during the whole war, only 321 U-boats attacked and at least damaged one or more Allied ships; this represented only about one-quarter of Dönitz's total submarine fleet, so c.850 boats never hit a single target. Individual command talent was everything, and war seems to have brought out that talent in only a small minority, usually those with long sea service behind them. (Author's collection)

During this period boats were sent out on independent patrols to a specific area on the map. Should German radio-intercept intelligence by the so-called B-Dienst detect shipping in that general area, a coded message would be sent to the nearest boat, ordering it to move to intercept. In the meantime boats would often endure lengthy periods of boring inactivity, patrolling what seemed like an empty ocean, listening to other boats receiving orders to attack and hoping their chance would come next.

U-47 at Scapa Flow

That the occasional use of individual boats against specific targets could be highly successful was proved early in the war when U-47 (KL Günther Prien) managed to infiltrate the Royal Navy fleet anchorage at Scapa Flow in the Orkney Islands and sink the battleship HMS *Royal Oak*. This episode is too well known to warrant lengthy description here, but it did underline several significant factors, particularly the importance of expert navigation and boat-handling in shallow waters.

The entry into Scapa Flow commenced at around 11.30pm on the night of 13/14 October 1939; U-47 moved through Kirk Sound on the surface

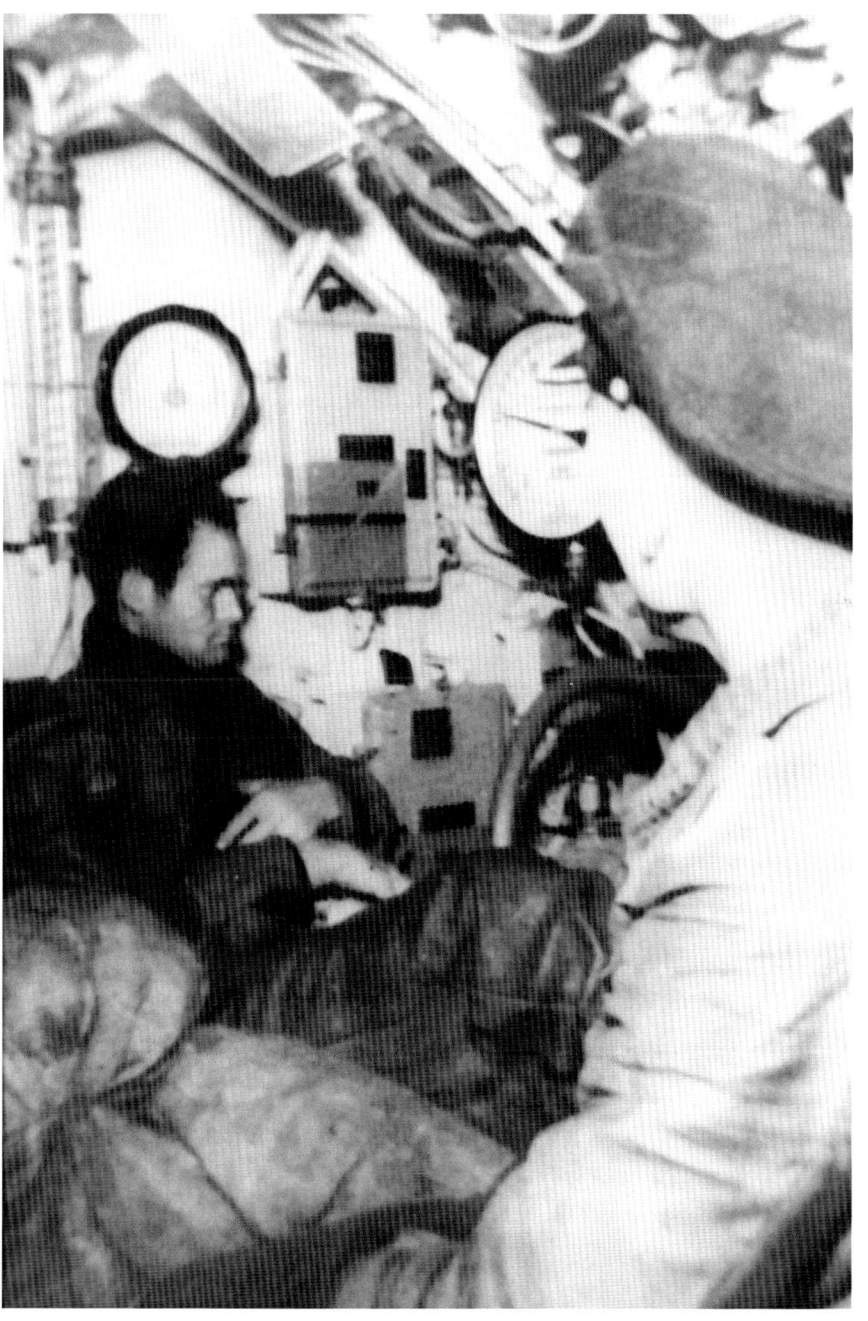

On the starboard side of the control room, above the boat's planesmen, a close watch is kept on the depth gauge. The average U-boat was exceptionally well built, and many survived dives to much greater depths than the recommended maximum. When KL Freiherr von Tiesenhausen's U-331 fired a salvo at HMS *Barham* on 24 November 1941, the sudden loss of the weight of four torpedoes made it difficult to control her trim, and her conning tower actually broke the surface ahead of the battleship HMS *Valiant*, which attempted to ram. The subsequent crash-dive was almost the undoing of U-331; with a faulty depth gauge, the boat plummeted past the estimated 'crush depth' of 100m (328ft), reaching an incredible 250m (820ft) before being brought under control. U-331 returned safely to Salamis in Greece on 21 February 1942. (Deutsches U-Boot Museum)

25

Even in the relatively empty waters of the South Atlantic, where lone U-boats hunted successfully from summer 1942, constant vigilance was expected of the bridge watch; sunny weather at least made this a relatively welcome duty. When operations by the ocean-going Type IXD-2 boats were extended in mid-1943 across the Indian Ocean to a base in Japanese-occupied Malaya, one factor was the hope of using returning boats to carry back to Germany a few tons of high-value strategic materials that were no longer getting through the Allied blockade of surface shipping. (Deutsches U-Boot Museum)

(though the cover of darkness was somewhat compromised by a display of the Aurora Borealis). The attack was timed to coincide with 'slack water' so that the boat's approach through the shallow channel would be assisted by the incoming flood tide, and the exit would be assisted by the ebb tide; even so, U-47's keel scraped along the bottom at one point, and the gap between two of the blockships barring the entrance to the sound was so narrow that she briefly became fouled on one of their anchor chains.

At 12.27am, U-47 finally entered the enormous harbour. Many warships were absent, and Prien spent over half an hour cruising around the anchorage looking for suitable targets, before launching his first two torpedoes at 12.58am. One failed to explode, and the other was detonated by hitting an anchor chain. Incredibly, this caused little visible reaction, so Prien coolly reloaded and fired again, to be rewarded by a massive explosion aboard the *Royal Oak*. Fortunately for Prien the British did not immediately suspect that a U-boat could have been responsible, but even without an active pursuit it took consummate skill from the submarine's navigator to take the boat back out through the narrow gap against a 10-knot cross current. Despite being briefly caught in the headlights of a vehicle passing on shore, the U-boat emerged safely into open water at around 2.15am on 14 October.

The Mediterannean: U-81 and U-331

The only other British battleship (in the strict sense of that term) to be sunk by U-boat action during World War II was also the victim of a single boat on a solo patrol.

U-boats had first penetrated into the dangerously shallow waters of the Mediterranean in late September 1941; by the following month 25 boats were in theatre, and in November two of them achieved notable results. The first, rather confused success came on 13 November when U-81 spotted the Royal Navy's Force H, which included the aircraft carrier HMS *Ark Royal* returning from delivering Hurricanes to Malta. Kapitänleutnant Friedrich Guggenberger fired torpedoes at long range, in fact aiming for the battleship HMS *Malaya*, but seems to have missed and hit the carrier;

meanwhile U-205 (KL Franz-Georg Reschke), which actually fired torpedoes at *Ark Royal*, missed her, and damaged *Malaya* – though not fatally. Although U-81 then suffered punishing depth-charge attacks by the escorts, Guggenberger eventually escaped. The carrier was still afloat, but could not be saved; she sank the following day 25 miles from Gibraltar during the attempt to tow her to safety.

Due to the delay between the torpedo hit and the eventual sinking, mercifully only one member of *Ark Royal*'s crew of around 1,600 men was lost; the outcome of an action 11 days later was tragically different. After landing German agents behind British lines in North Africa, U-331 (KL Hans-Diederich Freiherr von Tiesenhausen) had then set off to patrol eastwards towards the British Mediterranean Fleet base at Alexandria in Egypt. While submerged off Sidi Barrani on 25 November the boat's sonar picked up the sound of multiple ships' screws, and Baron Tiesenhausen's pursuit was soon rewarded with the sight through his periscope of three RN battleships (HMS *Barham*, *Valiant* and *Queen Elizabeth*) with a heavy destroyer escort. Tiesenhausen managed to slip through the destroyer screen undetected, and at a depth of about 23m (75ft) he fired a spread of four torpedoes at *Barham*'s port side from 1,200 metres. Three of them hit the battleship with devastating effect; she quickly turned on her side, and was destroyed by a massive boiler or magazine explosion, taking 862 of her crew with her when she sank only about four minutes after being hit.

NORTH AMERICAN WATERS, 1942

As the war progressed and the Atlantic convoy system matured there were fewer opportunities for attacks against merchantmen sailing independently. However, the German declaration of war against the USA in December 1941 brought the opportunity to engage a whole new range of targets. For the first half of 1942 the American precautions against submarine attack were quite

Fuel, stores and torpedo stowage was the governing factor for patrol endurance in distant waters. Everything that entered a U-boat had to be manoeuvred aboard through narrow hatches; here, the round hatch cover with a white-painted interior leads through into the pressure hull, while the elongated hatch is the access to the storage areas under the wooden decking. (Incidentally, the crates contain fruit drinks, not alcohol.) At the start of a patrol every spare corner inside the hull, including one of the two toilets, was crammed with stores; as the weeks passed things became slightly less crowded, but even smellier – in the dank interior of a submarine fresh food did not last long. (Deutsches U-Boot Museum)

The advent of the ten 1,688-ton Type XIV tanker/cargo U-boats, the so-called *Milch-Kuhe*, greatly increased the tactical usefulness of the Type VII boats for long-range work; here two have rendezvoused with a 'Milk-Cow' in the South Atlantic for refuelling. The 'cows' could carry 440 tons of fuel oil (enough to completely refill the tanks of two other boats from empty, or to generously 'top up' several more), plus four torpedoes, and tons of food – they even had baking-ovens for fresh bread. Unfortunately for Dönitz, from August 1942 code-breaking allowed the Allies to ambush and destroy them, mostly by air attack. Four had already been lost by July 1943, in which month alone four more were sunk; the ninth was destroyed that October, and the last – U-488 – by Allied warships in April 1944. (Deutsches U-Boot Museum)

inadequate, with masses of merchant shipping sailing independently and unescorted up and down the eastern coastal sealanes, including oil tankers from the Gulf of Mexico. The problem faced by Adm Dönitz was the insufficient numbers of U-boats available. The standard Type VIIC boats could cross the Atlantic, but their fuel reserves would not allow them to spend many weeks on patrol in target areas. The larger Type IX boats had greater range and endurance, but nowhere near sufficient numbers were ever available. The first wave sent to take the war into the waters off the US east coast in Operation 'Drumbeat' consisted of a mere six Type IXB and C boats: U-66, U-109, U-123, U-125, U-130 and U-502. Each commander was given freedom of action within a particular patrol area – a *Freijagd* – and eventually 21 boats saw action in these waters.

Kapitänleutnant Reinhard Hardegen in U-123, on his way to patrol the waters off New York, intercepted and sank the British freighter *Cyclops* south-east of Nova Scotia. This opened a U-boat campaign off the North American seaboard that became known as 'the Second Happy Time' for U-boat commanders, who benefited from a lack of AS precautions reminiscent of summer 1940–spring 1941. Not only were US ships still sailing fully illuminated and making free use of their radios, but there was no on-shore blackout to deny the U-boats navigation points. Some commanders even enjoyed the luxury of surfacing in daylight to sink ships with gunfire, which had become almost impossible in the eastern Atlantic. By the time he had expended his torpedo payload, KL Hardegen alone had claimed ten ships totalling around 66,100 tons.

Despite their limited range, a number of Type VIIC boats were also despatched to Canadian waters to intercept convoys off Nova Scotia along with two Type IX boats, and for a time these were equally successful. The US Navy and Coast Guard learned quickly, however, and the tactics of *Freijagd* could not last. Starting in the waters between Halifax and New York, an improving Allied ASW effort forced the U-boats steadily southwards into the Caribbean in search of easier prey. By July 1942 a convoy system was in place in the waters off the US eastern seaboard, and the new long-range Type

IXD-2 boats were mostly being deployed instead to the South Atlantic, ranging widely between the coasts of Africa and South America.

FAR EASTERN WATERS, 1943–44

It was sensible for U-boats to operate alone in these waters, and they continued to do so throughout the war. The shortage of ocean-going boats, combined with an initial lack of refuelling, resupply and repair facilities, dictated that the first steps in operating in such distant waters began in the South Atlantic and around the Cape of Good Hope up into the Indian Ocean, but with boats always returning to their bases on the French coast. By mid-1943, however, operations in the North Atlantic had become so perilous that, despite the paramount importance of these convoy routes, Dönitz decided to try operations further east – as the Japanese had suggested in December 1942.

The first so-called 'Monsoon Group' of 11 boats left French and Norwegian bases in July 1943, but only five reached their destination of Penang, Malaya, led by U-178 (KK Wilhelm Dommes, later KL Wilhelm Spahr); of a second group, only one survived the voyage. Allied shipping in the Indian Ocean at this time was still sailing independently and without escort, and the 'monsoon boat' commanders enjoyed relative freedom of action, sinking a total of about 70 vessels representing over 400,000 tons of shipping. However, the facilities made available by the Japanese were primitive, and despite KK Dommes' tireless activity as the shore-based flotilla commander his crews and their boats suffered badly, from health problems and a lack of spare parts respectively.

'WOLF-PACK' ATTACKS

The term 'wolf pack' has been used generically to describe any attack on shipping by several U-boats at the same time. In fact, the use of 'group' tactics preceded the specific, planned 'wolf pack' (*Rudeltaktik*) by some time, and there were several differences between the two doctrines. Admiral Dönitz was well aware of the potential advantages of employing U-boats offensively in groups – indeed, the possibility had been discussed in his flotilla during World War I. Although there is some dispute over who originated the *Rudeltaktik*, it certainly reached its full development under his command.

In the early part of the war, when a single U-boat spotted a convoy it would signal a report to BdU, which in turn would signal other nearby boats to join in the attack. Such group efforts, which were occurring as early as the late months of 1939, were an unco-ordinated series of individual attacks. There was no direct contact between boats, but each would keep abreast of events by listening in to wireless traffic between other boats and BdU. The 'pack' therefore existed only during the actual attack, and dispersed immediately afterwards. (It should be remembered that in 1940 Dönitz seldom had more than about 20 Type VII boats at sea simultaneously.)

It is interesting to note the official Kriegsmarine view (as of 1943) regarding attacks by more than one U-boat: 'The fundamental purpose of the U-boat in naval tactics is to operate alone… As a result, there is no such thing as concentrating U-boats for the purpose of co-operating and supporting each other in collective actions. From the point at which a group

(continued on page 32)

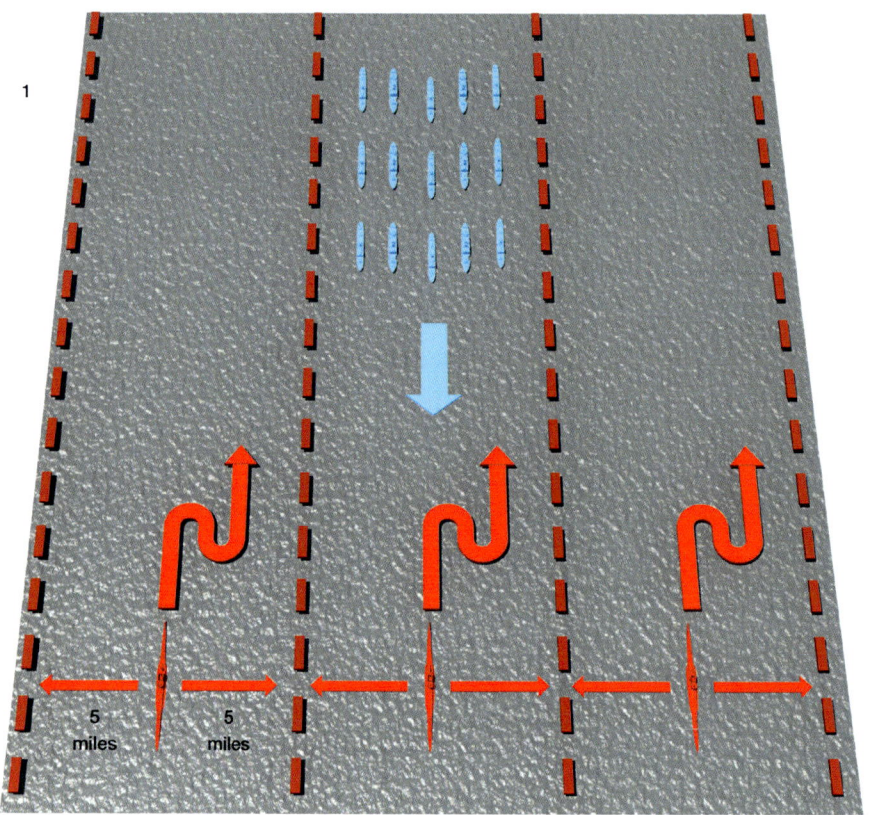
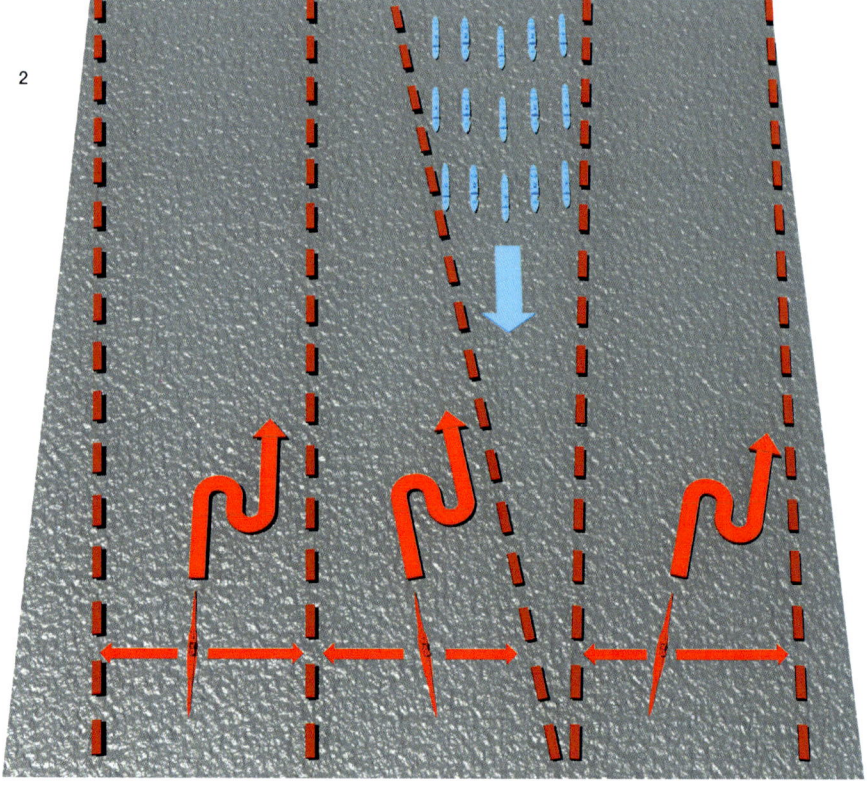

These photos give some small idea of typical conditions in the North Atlantic. During long patrols on the surface, crews spent day after day in heavy swells while the U-boat rolled and pitched uncontrollably, with little hope of sighting Allied shipping. In true storm conditions the boats had to submerge. (Deutsches U-Boot Museum, and author's collection)

D **U-BOAT PATROL/REPORTING LINE**
(Not to scale.)

1: The theory
Three U-boats of a patrol line (which might number up to 20 boats) are positioned to exploit the bridge watches' maximum visual range between each pair of boats – c.5 miles each, thus 10 miles. Each has its own navigational 'lane', up which it patrols on a weaving course. With no gaps in visibility, and the submarines shifting course laterally as well as sailing forwards, a wide area of ocean can be covered, within which no Allied shipping should be able to slip past unnoticed.

2: The more likely reality
While that scenario might be possible to maintain in calm seas and good visibility, such conditions were not often found in the North Atlantic. Even when sufficient boats were available for a wide line, foul weather, strong currents, heavy seas, and cloud cover could deny the U-boats' navigators a chance to take sextant readings for days on end, so it was all too easy to drift off course. Here the boat at the centre has drifted to port slightly, and the boat at the right has drifted to starboard, opening up a gap between them. Over the considerable distance covered in a day or two's sailing this gap could widen into a segment broad enough for even a small convoy – let alone an Allied merchantman sailing alone – to slip past the patrol line unreported.

Accurate navigation depended on being able to surface to fix the boat's position by taking celestial readings with a sextant. Unlike Allied practice, in U-boats navigation was the responsibility not of a commissioned officer but of a senior non-commissioned rating, the *Obersteuermann* or coxswain. Stormy weather with heavy cloud cover made it impossible to 'shoot the sun', and in heavy seas and strong currents boats could easily drift off course, opening wide gaps in a 'wolf pack's' grid of patrol lanes. (Deutsches U-Boot Museum)

of U-boats go into action, each submarine acts, as before, as a separate and individual unit....'

Such engagements against the same convoy, at the same time, by a number of submarine commanders acting individually, had clear disadvantages. Most obviously, valuable torpedoes might be wasted when more than one boat attacked the same vessel, and it was difficult to keep an accurate record of the results obtained by each boat.

Patrol/reporting lines

The move towards organized 'pack' attacks came with the introduction of patrol or reporting lines. Initially this would involve a group of boats patrolling in line abreast. The distance between the boats would theoretically be set at twice the distance of visibility from any boat's conning tower (about 8km or 5 miles from each), so that the mid-line of this roughly 10-mile gap between two adjacent boats would be at their limits of visibility. In this way it should be impossible for an Allied ship to pass through the gap between two boats without being spotted.

This patrol line would motor on the surface astride the anticipated course of the convoy at relatively slow speed, thus covering the whole area of ocean between the outer limits of visibility from the first and the last boat in the line. If a convoy was spotted and reported by any boat, all the boats in the patrol line could theoretically be vectored against it to cause the maximum losses. However, even when a good number of boats were employed, if the course of the convoy was incorrectly estimated or if it changed course, then even a large convoy could escape interception in the vast expanse of the North Atlantic.

There were also difficulties simply in maintaining the patrol line. In calm weather and good visibility it was relatively easy for each boat to maintain its course in relation to other boats in the line; but in stormy weather, with heavy cloud cover and rough seas, it was only too easy for a boat to wander off course. Since the intervals between them were set at the limits of visibility, even a slight deviation from course could result in a gap in the visual surveillance. Bad weather would often force boats to travel submerged, and storms lasting several days – hardly a rarity in the North Atlantic – would prevent a boat's navigator from confirming his position by taking sextant readings; huge gaps could open up between some boats, while others could end up almost on top of one another. The numbers of operational boats available meant that this far from ideal situation was the best that could be hoped for.

Significant successes were achieved by these early tactics, however. On 20 September 1940, convoy HX-72 was sighted by U-47 (see under 'The Kretschmer method', above). The sighting was reported back to BdU, which ordered an eventual total of nine boats into the attack. Of these, five – U-32, U-47, U-48, U-99 and U-100 – succeeded in actually engaging the convoy.

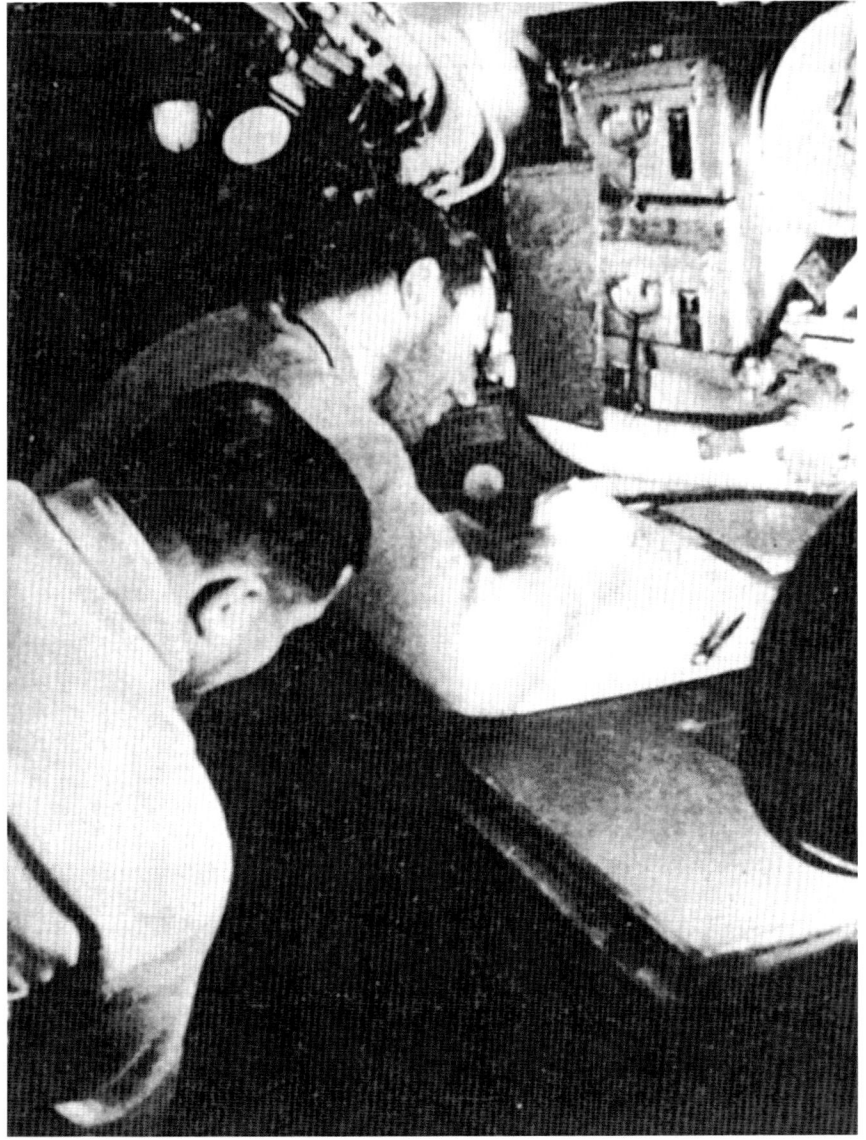

In the dimly lit control room, the *Obersteuermann* at the map table plots a course for the next leg of the U-boat's patrol. His status recalled that historically held by a ship's 'master' and other technical 'warrant officers', separate from the line officers. On a U-boat he often doubled as the third watch-keeping officer, 'IIIWO'. (Author's collection)

U-32 and U-47 torpedoed and damaged one ship each; U-48 sank one and damaged another; U-99 sank three, and U-100 (KL Joachim Schepke) sank no fewer than seven – a total of 11 ships sunk, representing 72,700 tons.

On 16 October 1940 the *Trevisa*, a straggler from convoy SC-7, was sunk by U-124. The next day, in the Western Approaches, U-38 sank another straggler, the *Aenos*, and U-48 intercepted the main convoy, sinking the *Scoresby* and the tanker *Languedoc*. Alerted to the convoy's position by U-48, BdU ordered others into action, and on 18 October U-46, U-99, U-100, U-101 and U-123 joined the attack. U-46 sank three ships, and U-99 six; U-100 torpedoed and damaged three, U-101 sank three and damaged one, and U-123 sank four – a total of no fewer than 20 ships sunk from a convoy of 35, representing almost 80,000 tons.

* * *

These early, successful convoy battles took place during a period when British and Canadian ASW strength and tactics were in their relative infancy, but this 'Happy Time' would not last long. The Allies soon developed effective tactics, and this shift in the balance was dramatized during ten days of March 1941, when four commanders – including three of Germany's top U-boat 'aces', Prien, Schepke and Kretschmer – were all either killed or captured with their crews. The largely unco-ordinated group attacks could no longer be depended upon to bring success. One factor that impacted on the success of these patrol lines, and of which the Germans had no knowledge, was, of course, the success of the British decryption experts at Bletchley Park in breaking the intercepted coded signals traffic, using the 'Enigma' automatic encryption machine, between BdU in France and its operational boats. Thanks to this priceless intelligence, the Admiralty often knew exactly which areas the U-boats were patrolling, and could thus route convoys to avoid them (despite the fact that the German B-Dienst had broken a code used by Allied merchant shipping).

E: 'WOLF-PACK' ATTACKS

1: Typical patrol lines, autumn 1941 On 28 August 1941 a 'wolf pack' with the codename Gruppe 'Markgraf' was carrying out a patrol along the route labelled **(1)**. It consisted initially of 14 boats, with five more joining later. Allied intelligence was aware of their presence but not their exact location. Convoy SC-42 **(track A)**, consisting of 64 freighters escorted by just one destroyer and three corvettes, was unable to re-route further north because of pack ice; on 9 September the convoy was spotted by U-85 (Olt z S Eberhard Greger), and the attacks began. Over the next two days a total of 17 merchantmen were torpedoed, with two more stragglers being hit by U-boats on 16 and 19 September. A total of 68,260 tons of shipping was sunk, and 14,130 tons damaged. No U-boats were lost.

On 15 October, convoy SC-48 **(track B)** passed through a second U-boat patrol area, and was intercepted by a number of boats including some from a pack codenamed Gruppe 'Mordbrenner' **(2)**. A total of about 13 boats intercepted the 52-odd ships; despite a much heavier escort consisting of a destroyer and seven corvettes, the attackers succeeded in sinking nine merchantmen and two warships, totalling just under 50,000 tons.

2 & 3: Torpedo guidance systems, 1942 & 1944 These 1941 successes were achieved with conventional unguided torpedoes; later, U-boats would be provided with torpedoes fitted with the FAT and LUT pre-set steering systems.

(2) shows a FAT-guided torpedo fired from the flank of a convoy (in fact the U-boat would be ahead of its beam, not level, since torpedoes were fired at a convergence-point ahead of the target's course). The torpedo would follow a straight course until it reached the flank of the target, then turn 90 degrees, then make a series of 180-degree turns until it met a ship or ran out of power.

(3) With LUT the boat did not have to be at right-angles when it fired, but could be on any heading relative to the convoy's course. The torpedo made a straight run, then another at 90 degrees, and finally made a series of 180-degree turns until it acquired a target (by this time the convoy would be occupying the same area of ocean as the torpedo's weaving course).

4: Bridge watch The minimum watch was the duty watch officer and four seamen, each maintaining a vigilant binocular watch over his assigned quarter, for up to four hours at a time. Periscopes would not be raised during such surface watches, to help avoid the submarine itself being spotted.

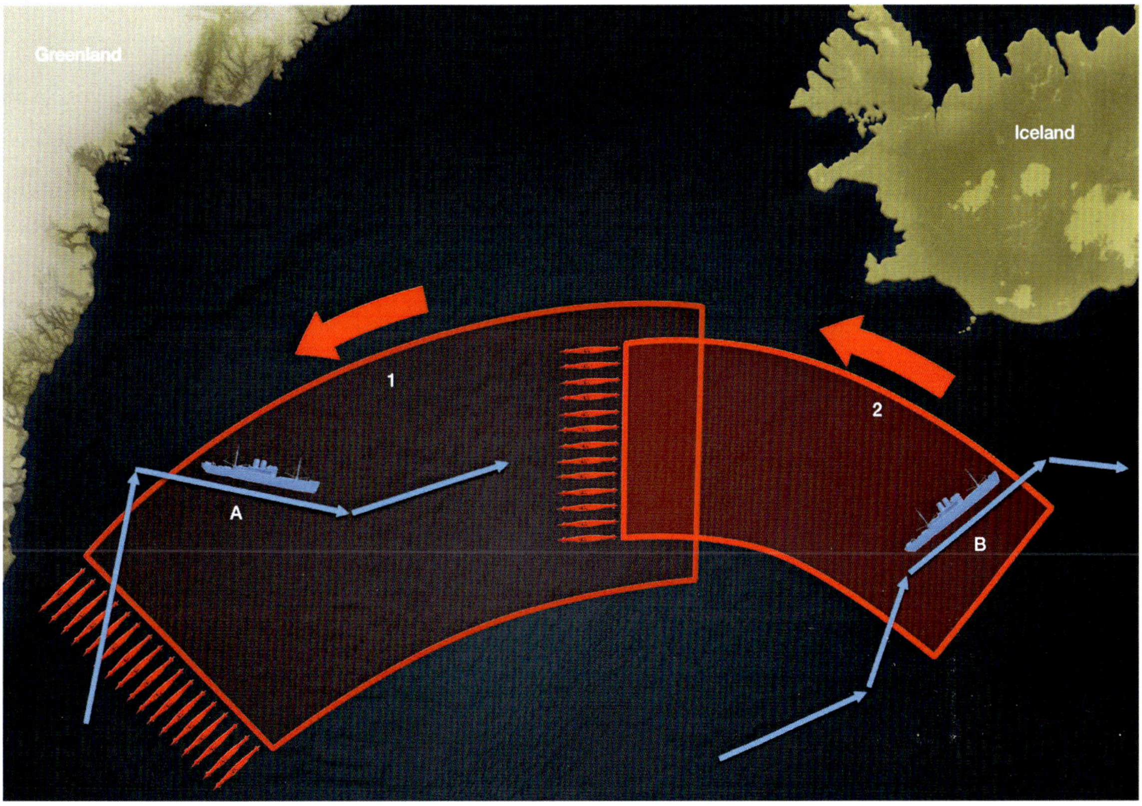

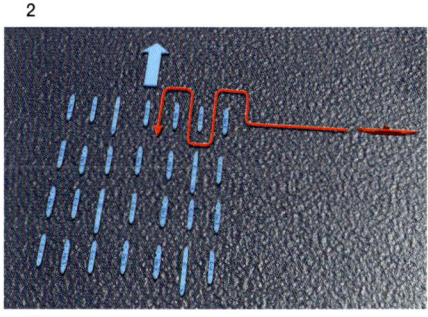
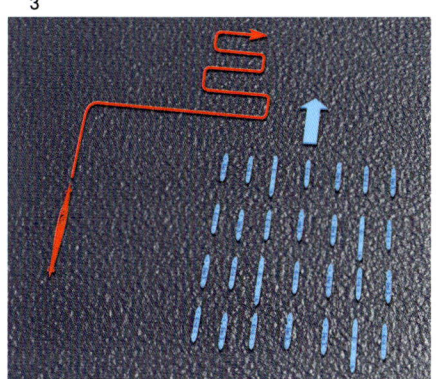

Many propaganda photos were taken of U-boat commanders at the 'sky' periscope in the relatively large control room – see page 4. The smaller 'attack' periscope used during an actual engagement was one level higher, inside the conning tower, where there was no room for a photographer. This is a view up through the hatchway from the control room into the tower, showing a commander at the attack periscope. (Author's collection)

Fast patrol lines

As many more boats became available to Dönitz a greatly improved method could be introduced, the so-called 'fast patrol lines'. These multiple reporting lines could cover a far greater area, and the speed at which they moved meant that it was less likely that they would be detected and located. Their first major success came on the night of 9 September 1941, when the large convoy SC-42 was intercepted. Of its 70 ships, about 20 were sunk (claims range between 16 and 22).

After an initial unsuccessful attack by U-85, the carnage began when U-432 sank the 5,200-ton ore-carrier *Muneric*. U-652 joined the battle, torpedoing the freighter *Baron Pentland* and the tanker *Tahchee*; U-432 then sank the Dutch *Winterswijk* and the Norwegian *Stargard*, U-81 torpedoed the freighter *Sally Maersk*, and U-82 the catapult-armed merchantman *Empire Hudson*.

Next day British lookouts were making multiple sightings of U-boat periscopes, and before long U-85 had added the freighter *Thistleglen* to the growing list of victims; U-82 then sank both the *Gypsum Queen* and the tanker *Bulysses*. Not everything went in the Germans' favour, however: U-501 (KK Hugo Förster) was caught on the surface by the corvettes HMCS *Chambly* and HMCS *Moose Jaw*, and first depth-charged, then rammed, though most of her crew survived to be rescued by the Canadian warships. Meanwhile, U-207 had torpedoed the freighters *Berury* and *Stonepool*, U-432 the Swedish freighter *Garm*, and U-82 the freighter *Empire Crossbill* and the Swedish *Scania*. The final loss to convoy SC-42 came on 16 September, when the freighter *Jedmore* was sunk by U-98. A total of over 62,600 tons of shipping had been sunk, to say nothing of the vast amount of cargo that they carried to the bottom.

The turn of the tide

The true 'year of the wolf pack' was 1942, during which the U-Boat Arm sank nearly 8 million tons of Allied shipping in the Atlantic. By the winter of 1942/43, Dönitz had some 200–230 operational boats, of which about 70–100 were usually on patrol simultaneously. Many Allied naval and air assets were diverted from the North Atlantic to support the Anglo-American 'Torch' landings in

French North Africa and subsequent operations in the Mediterranean, and in November 1942 alone the 'wolf packs' sank 117 ships, although the appalling weather of that winter would hamper the efforts of both sides thereafter.

Some massive convoy battles took place in March 1943, when for three weeks a change in Kriegsmarine ciphers interrupted the flow of 'Ultra' intelligence. However, in May a combination of new Allied strength at sea and in the air, and new and much more effective centimetric radar technology – whose possibility the Germans had never even suspected – suddenly shifted the balance (see above, 'Basic Chronology' panel, page 6). Between 28 April and 6 May, no fewer than 53 boats of Gruppen 'Star', 'Fink' and 'Amsel' were vectored towards the 43-ship convoy ONS-5, which was disorganized and slowed by foul weather. They sank 17 merchantmen totalling c.62,000 tons, but thick fog then provided cover for the convoy on 5/6 May. Escort Group B7, with elements of Support Groups 1 and 3 sent out from Newfoundland, plus long-range aircraft, sank seven U-boats, and an eighth was lost to air attack while limping home damaged. This last fell victim to a simultaneous Allied air campaign that saw regular patrols combing the Bay of Biscay astride the U-boats' routes from and to their bases. By day these were flights of fast, heavily armed RAF Mosquitoes and Beaufighters; by night, bombers equipped with centimetric radar, 'Leigh Light' searchlights and shallow-set depth charges could often attack faster than a submarine could dive.

The battle for ONS-5 heralded the defeat of the 'wolf-pack' tactics; the new Allied short-wave radar sets had virtually robbed the U-boats of their ability to operate on the surface, day or night, without attracting Allied aircraft and warships, and when forced 'into the cellar' they were unable to manoeuvre fast enough to ambush potential targets. A total of c.96 boats were lost in May–July 1943; Dönitz withdrew them from the North Atlantic on 24 May, standing down the 'wolf packs' until the autumn. Their return failed to regain the lost initiative that winter, and the last, Gruppe 'Preussen', was finally dissolved on 22 March 1944.

Focke Wulf Fw 200C-1 Condor reconnaissance-bomber of I/KG 40, probably photographed at Bordeaux-Merignac, from which base that Gruppe flew wide patrol circuits over the Bay of Biscay and the Atlantic west of Ireland, staging at Norwegian airfields. The bombload of this converted airliner was five 250kg/550lb bombs; it carried a 20mm cannon for strafing, and three 7.92mm machine guns for air-to-air defence. Notable anti-shipping successes included Olt Jope's sinking of the fast 42,000-ton liner *Empress of Britain* on 26 October 1940. (Author's collection)

KRIEGSMARINE-LUFTWAFFE CO-OPERATION

The insistence of Reichsmarschall Hermann Göring that 'everything that flew' belonged to him, and consequent inter-service rivalry, would mean that despite the potential for success, co-operation between the Kriegsmarine and Luftwaffe would sometimes be problematic. Although Luftwaffe anti-shipping operations were often very successful, nevertheless instances of close inter-service co-operation were relatively rare. (In early 1940 one notorious example of lack of communication between the two services led to Luftwaffe bombers on an anti-shipping strike sinking a Kriegsmarine destroyer, the *Leberecht Maas*; a second destroyer, *Max Schultz*, which moved in to rescue the survivors, hit a mine and also sank, bringing the total

Before the first of the escort carriers became available to convoys late in 1941, close aerial protection depended on the so-called 'CAM-ships' – Catapult Armed Merchantmen. There was no means of recovering the Hurricane fighter once it had been launched, and after his one-and-only mission the pilot had to ditch or parachute into the sea, hoping to be recovered before he drowned or froze to death. (Library and Archives Canada/Dept. National Defence Collection/PA-105735)

loss of life to 578 sailors. Neither the Luftwaffe nor the Kriegsmarine units had been informed of the others' presence in the area.)

The Fw 200C Condor

There were, however, episodes of inter-service co-operation that did impact on the U-boat war. After the fall of France in summer 1940 the Luftwaffe, like the U-Bootwaffe, gained a number of forward bases on the Atlantic coast, and among the aircraft operated from these were the four-engined Focke-Wulf Fw 200C Condors of I/Kampfgeschwader 40. Starting in August 1940, these enjoyed considerable success in attacking Allied shipping in the Bay of Biscay and out into the Atlantic, sinking 90,000 tons in August–September, and 85 ships totalling 363,000 tons by early February 1941.

However, the Fw 200 was being asked to perform well beyond its capabilities; initially designed as a passenger airliner and hastily adapted for military use, it soon demonstrated that its airframe was too weak for the stresses of combat flying. It was notorious for breaking its back in heavy landings, and strenuous evasive manoeuvres to avoid Allied fighters could tear off a wing. In mid-1941 it was decided to relegate the Condors to locating and shadowing convoys while transmitting homing signals to guide U-boats towards them. The results were poorer than they might have been had a truly integrated naval and air command been established. Any convoys spotted by the Condors had to be reported first up the Luftwaffe chain of command, and only then to the Kriegsmarine. It might take a full 24 hours between a convoy being sighted and BdU being informed, by which time it might be too late for U-boats to be vectored on the target effectively.

The system did have its successes, however. In July 1941 the formation of convoy OG-69 had been detected by German radio intelligence, and aircraft were despatched to try to locate the ships. The convoy was spotted by a Condor, and a group of eight U-boats were directed to the area to intercept, while relays of Fw 200s shadowed the ships. Guided by the aircraft, U-68 located the convoy on 26 July; the first attack was made the following day by U-79, and others were launched by U-126, U-203 and U-561. These resulted in eight ships being sunk – though since all were small freighters, the total of just over 11,000 tons was a meagre reward for all the effort.

The advent in 1941 of the CAM-ships (Catapult Armed Merchantmen, carrying a single Hurricane fighter for a desperate one-way mission), and later of small escort aircraft carriers converted from merchant vessel hulls, began to give convoys their own integral air cover. The first Condor was shot down on 3 August 1941 by a CAM-ship Hurricane flown by Lt Everett from HMS *Maplin*; over convoy OG-74 the following month another was lost to a Wildcat from the first of the new escort carriers, HMS *Audacity*; and in mid-December, while escorting convoy HG-76, *Audacity*'s pilots shot down two more Fw 200s. The Condor's role became increasingly hazardous, and after the battle for the Arctic convoy PQ-18 in October 1942 they were withdrawn from Atlantic operations.

Combined air-sea strikes

Occasional combined operations by the Luftwaffe and Kriegsmarine did achieve considerable success, one example being the attacks on the notorious convoy PQ-17. Sailing from Iceland to Murmansk in northern Russia, this convoy of 36 (mostly American) ships is estimated to have carried enough military hardware to equip more than 50,000 troops. On 27 June 1942 the convoy departed Reykjavik with a fairly heavy escort, and a strong Royal Navy surface force was in distant cover. The convoy was spotted by a Condor of 3/ KG 40 on 1 July, and nine U-boats were vectored towards it,

Looking forward along the deck of a Type VII boat, 'iced up' on a patrol in northern waters; note the 8.8cm deck gun. Due to the limited life of the U-boat's batteries before they needed recharging, boats would run on the surface as much as possible wherever it was judged safe to do so, whatever the weather. Operations against the Arctic convoys to North Russia were as difficult for the U-boats as for the Allied escorts. In winter the bridge watch suffered from extreme cold, and the short daylight hours, rough seas and bad visibility made observation very difficult; in summer, the long hours of daylight gave a surfaced boat no cover. (Deutsches U-Boot Museum)

led by U-255 (KL Reinhardt Reche). On 2–3 July a strong German surface force including the *Tirpitz*, *Lützow* and *Admiral Scheer* also set sail to intercept. On 4–5 July, Luftwaffe attacks by He 111s of KG 26 and Ju 88s of KG 30 sank five ships. Unaware that the German battleship and cruiser squadron had been recalled in the meantime, and expecting a major surface action, the Admiralty sent orders for PQ-17's destroyer escort to steam to join the RN heavy squadron, and for the convoy and its smaller escorts, such as armed trawlers and minesweepers, to scatter. The hapless merchantmen were picked off one by one; by nightfall on 7 July the Luftwaffe bombers had flown more than 200 sorties and sunk a total of eight ships (40,300 tons), and by 15 July the U-boats had sunk another 16 – a total loss of 24 out of 36 ships (142,500 tons), plus some 100,000 tons of cargo including more than 400 tanks, 3,300 other vehicles and 200 aircraft.

Fortunately for the Allies, Luftwaffe/Kriegsmarine co-operation would never again achieve comparable success. For instance, on 15 November 1943 a Bv 222 flying boat located convoy MKS-30, and three separate 'reporting lines' of U-boats were laid across its correctly anticipated route. Despite this convoy being joined by another, SL-139 – thus creating a major target consisting of 73 vessels including escorts – not a single ship was sunk by U-boats, despite numerous attempts between 18 and 21 November. The Luftwaffe also launched an attack on the convoy by more than 20 Heinkel He 177 heavy bombers, which sank one small ship and damaged a second; the U-boats did manage to shoot down two Allied aircraft and damage one ship, but these successes were negligible compared with the German losses of three U-boats and five aircraft.

ASSOCIATED EQUIPMENT

Bachstelze ('Wagtail')

The *Bachstelze* was an attempt to increase the visual range of a U-boat when operating on the surface. Because a submarine sat relatively low in the water, the bridge at the top of the conning tower gave its watch personnel only a limited range of visibility, even with first-class optical equipment. The greater visual range of lookouts high in the crow's nest of a surface ship might allow warships to surprise a U-boat on the surface before it had time to dive.

Manufactured by Focke-Achgelis, the Fa 330 Bachstelze was an unpowered gyrocopter – in essence, a rotary-winged kite. Simply manufactured from metal tubing, with a seat for a pilot and a small pedal-operated rudder, it could be carried disassembled in watertight containers on the 'winter garden' Flak platform behind a submarine's conning tower, and quickly assembled on a small platform mounted on the rail. It was tethered to the submarine by a winch cable; with the U-boat running at speed on the surface, the 'slipstream' would spin the rotors of the Bachstelze, allowing it to lift off – a speed of only 17km/h (10.5mph) into a moderate headwind would keep the craft aloft. The Bachstelze could attain an altitude of around 120m (400ft), and increased the visual range from the U-boat from the 8km (5 mile) norm of the bridge lookouts to about 40km (25 miles); the pilot could communicate with the submarine by telephone. After use the Bachstelze was simply winched back down to its platform and disassembled for stowing.

The problem with the Bachstelze was the time it took to recover it if an Allied aircraft spotted the submarine. In such circumstances the U-boat had to

This rare shot shows a *Bachstelze* gyrocopter assembled on its special platform on the rear rail of the 'winter garden' of a Type IX U-boat (the pale band painted around the upper forward part of the conning tower indicates that this photo was taken during exercises, not on operations). A number of these rare craft survived the war, and examples may be seen in the Imperial War Museum at Duxford in England, the National Museum of the US Air Force at Dayton, Ohio, USA, and the Deutsches Technikmuseum in Berlin, Germany. (Deutsches U-Boot Museum)

crash-dive, and the tethering cable would be jettisoned. The kite was fitted with a parachute in the hope that the pilot might be able to make a safe descent; the (extremely optimistic) theory was that the U-boat might be able to surface once danger had passed, to find and recover him. Around 200 Bachstelze were built, but their very moderate success led to their use being discontinued.

Apart from the potentially sacrificial aspect, the theory of the towed observation kite was perfectly practical; but in fact only one merchant ship is known to have been sucessfully intercepted by the use of an Fa 330 – the Greek-registered *Efthalia Mari*, sunk by U-177 on 6 August 1943 in the Indian Ocean off Madagascar (see Plate F). This Type IXD-2 boat, commanded from April 1942 by the 'ace' KK Robert Gysae, sailed on her second patrol on 1 April 1943 as one of a group of seven boats operating at first off Cape Town, and then into the Indian Ocean. (She had sunk four

This photo taken during the 1944 commissioning ceremony for the Type IXD boat U-873 (KL Freidrich Steinhoff) is interesting in that it clearly shows not only the extent of the lower rear Flak platform, but also (upper left, just below the jack) the small grilled plate fixed to the rail of the upper platform, on which the *Bachstelze* was assembled. The aft Flak weapon has not yet been mounted, but note the water- and pressure-proof lockers for ready-use ammunition. (Deutsches U-Boot Museum)

U-295 (KL Wieboldt), one of the Type VII boats specially adapted to act as mother-ships for midget submarines, here carrying two *Biber* submersibles on special cradles on her fore and aft decks; note their externally clamped torpedoes. An operation on 5–8 January 1945 by three such modified U-boats, with the aim of sinking a Soviet battleship at anchor, was aborted, and was anyway of very questionable usefulness. Even if it had succeeded, the loss of one elderly battleship would have had an entirely insignificant effect on the Soviet war effort, at best providing a minor propaganda coup at a time when Germany was suffering crushing military setbacks on all fronts. (Deutsches U-Boot Museum)

ships between 28 May and 29 July, but the *Efthalia Mari* was the first and only interception made using the Bachstelze, despite many launches.) The first inkling the Allies got of the Bachstelze's existence came in May 1944, when another Type IXD-2, U-852, was located on the surface in the Indian Ocean by an RAF Wellington. Attacking as the U-boat attempted to dive, the bomber inflicted enough damage to force her to the surface; when additional aircraft joined in the attack she was damaged so badly that KL Heinz-Wilhelm Eck was forced to run her aground on a beach on the coast of Somaliland. Demolition charges rendered U-852 unsalvageable, but among the items the Allies recovered from the wreck was her Bachstelze.

U-boats as midget-submarine mother ships

In the last months of the war an operation was planned to sink the Soviet battleship *Archangelsk* (the former HMS *Royal Sovereign*), which was anchored in the Kola Inlet east of Murmansk. It was planned that the Type VII boats U-295, U-716 and U-992 would each carry two *Biber*-type midget submarines, one on the foredeck and another aft.[2] Released at the mouth of the inlet, the six Bibers, each with two torpedoes, would then enter the bay independently to sink the battleship.

The force duly left Norway on 5 January 1945, and almost immediately encountered a number of problems. The Biber, like all midget submarines, was designed to operate in relatively shallow coastal waters, and when the Type VIIs carrying them dived the Bibers were unable to withstand the water pressures of the greater depths at which U-boats normally operated. Their

[2] For notes on *Biber* and other German midget submarines, see Elite 177: *German Special Forces of World War II*.

portholes were fractured, badly affecting the buoyancy of the Type VII mother-ships, and the mechanisms holding the Bibers' external torpedoes were also damaged. With the chances of success reduced to almost zero, the force returned to its base on 8 January.

OFFENSIVE WEAPONS

TORPEDOES

The basic German torpedo used on submarines during most of the war was the G7e (with a suffix indicating the specific version, e.g. G7e T4) and before 1943 this was a fairly simple weapon. As with any projectile fired at a moving target, the commander would estimate the distance to the target, its heading and its speed, and aim the torpedo at a point ahead of it where ship and torpedo were calculated to meet. If this was successful, the warhead would be detonated by a dual trigger mechanism initiated by either impact or the ship's magnetic field. The very high percentage of failures that bedevilled commanders in 1940 were found to be due to the unanticipated effects of high air pressure inside the submarines on depth-setting mechanisms and the magnetic triggers, and careless quality control during acceptance tests of contact triggers.

Once these problems had been solved, by about March 1941, the system was perfectly adequate when the U-boat crew had plenty of time to prepare an attack without much danger of Allied interruption. (Even so, it should be noted that far more torpedoes were fired than ever hit a target. A post-war analysis of attacks made by the most successful individual U-boat of the war, U-48, operational September 1939–August 1943, produced a figure of only 55 hits from 126 torpedo launches – 44 hits from 96 surface launches, and 11 hits from 30 submerged launches.) As the war progressed, however, submariners often had to contend with trying to avoid the attentions of increasingly

A G7 torpedo being loaded aboard a Type VII U-boat in dock; note that the detonating mechanism has not yet been inserted. The standard ordnance for most of the war was the G7e, 53.3cm (21in) in diameter and 7.16m (23ft 6in) long, with a 280kg (616lb) high-explosive warhead. Launched from the tube by compressed air, and powered by a 100hp electric motor – in place of the earlier G7a's compressed-air-powered propeller, which left a trail of bubbles – the G7e had a speed of some 30 knots (56km/h, 34.5mph) and a range – in its T3 version – of up to 7.5km (4.6 miles). (Deutsches U-Boot Museum)

numerous and well-directed Allied escort ships as the same time as calculating and delivering their attacks. New technology was accordingly developed at the Experimental Torpedo Station (Torpedoversuchsanstalt) at Gotenhafen.

G7e T4 *Falke* ('Falcon')

This was the first of the acoustic or 'homing' torpedoes to be introduced; once fired, the torpedo would home in on the cavitation noise caused by a ship's propeller. Since it was specifically designed for use against merchantmen, which usually travelled in convoy at less than 10 knots, it was permitted to have a lower running speed (20 knots) than the previous G7e variants. Introduced in March 1943, the G7e T4 found almost immediate success when used in attacks on convoy HX-229 by U-221, U-603 and U-758. U-221 succeeded in sinking the *Walter Q. Gresham* and the *Canadian Star;* U-603 sank the *Elin K.*, and U-758 sank the *Zaanland* and damaged the *James Oglethorpe* (later finished off by another boat). In total, about 30,000 tons of shipping had been destroyed by the new T4 during these actions.

G7e T5 *Zaunkönig* ('Wren')

The T4 remained in service only briefly before being replaced by the improved T5, with a slightly increased running speed of around 25 knots and a longer range. This type was specifically designed to be effective against escorting warships, so its homing device was set to react to the cavitation frequency of a smaller, faster warship steaming at 10–18 knots.

The T5 was first used in September 1943, against convoy ONS-18. During the attacks of 20 September the frigate HMS *Langan* and the destroyer HMS *St. Croix* were hit and damaged beyond repair with T5s fired by U-270 and U-338 respectively. When the frigate HMS *Itchen* and corvette HMS *Polyanthus* arrived on the scene to offer help the latter was hit and sunk with a T5 fired by U-952. At around midnight on the following day the *Itchen*

A torpedo is seen here being loaded through the forward hatch directly into the forward torpedo compartment. Note the special trestles and other equipment required for manoeuvring its 1.5-ton weight in confined spaces. Manhandling torpedoes was awkward enough in harbour, let alone at sea when transferring 'eels' into the boat from their stowage under the deck outside the pressure hull. In total, a Type VII boat could carry no more than 14 torpedoes, and a Type IX a maximum of 24, usually 22. (Deutsches U-Boot Museum)

The upper pair of bow tubes were loaded by winching the torpedo up with chains and running it along a heavy steel overhead beam; to facilitate loading at sea the torpedoes were greased, and the boat was trimmed slightly bow-heavy. During patrols the torpedoes had to be withdrawn for overhaul every four or five days, one usually being 'pulled' each day so the other tubes remained ready for use. Reloading a tube could take about an hour and a half, and could not be done without a good deal of noise; this was a real consideration when a boat had emptied its tubes but was still in the presence of the enemy. (Deutsches U-Boot Museum)

was hit by a T5 fired by U-666 and sank rapidly, leaving only three survivors. A number of merchantmen also fell victim to the T5 during these actions.

The Zaunkönig torpedo was used to some effect throughout the remainder of the war, but in fact of *c*.700 acoustic torpedoes launched, fewer than 80 destroyed a ship. There were several drawbacks to their use. Firstly, in late 1943 the Allies were quick to devise a decoy known as 'Foxer'. This array of hollow, perforated tubes was towed several hundred metres astern of the warship. The swirling of the water around and through the tubes, and the tubes banging together, generated louder cavitation noises than the propellers, so the acoustic torpedo homed in on the Foxer and not the warship. (The drawback for the Allies was that the amount of noise created also rendered their own Asdic ineffective, thus helping to conceal any U-boat, and could also help other nearby U-boats home in on the convoy.)

The T5's detonator proved to be over-sensitive, often exploding the warhead when it simply encountered turbulent water; but a more deadly side-effect was that it was suspected of occasionally circling back on the boat that had fired it – at least two, U-377 and U-972, are believed to have been sunk by their own torpedoes. To counter this, commanders either dived immediately after firing a T5 from a bow tube, to a depth of at least 60m (200ft) – well below the operating depth of the torpedo; or switched to 'silent running' immediately after a shot from a stern tube.

Experiments were also conducted in the use of wire-guided torpedoes, resulting in the G7e **T10** *Spinne* ('**Spider**'), with a running speed of 30 knots and a range of 5,000m, but this type never entered service.

G7e T11
This improved version of the T5 Zaunkönig was developed late in the war, specifically to counter Foxer decoys. It was designed to be fired ahead of the Allied escort so that the first cavitation noises it detected would be the warship, not the Foxer towed far astern. It had not been fully introduced into service by the end of the war, but had certainly proceeded beyond experimental status; three such torpedoes were found on the U-534 when she

inset 1

inset 2

25 miles

5 miles

was raised from the Kattegat in 1993.[3] There are, however, no records of any Allied ship being sunk by a T11.

Torpedo guidance systems:
FAT *(Federapparat Torpedo)*
This was the earlier of two types of steering device that could be fitted to a standard G7e T3 torpedo, which had the effect of regularly altering its course by 180 degrees after an initial straight run. When fired by a boat 'aimed' at right angles to the flank of a convoy, the torpedo would first run straight towards it, and then alter course to meander through the lanes of ships, repeatedly altering course by 180 degrees, until it either hit a target or ran out of power; each 'leg' of the course could be set to between 800m and 1,500 metres. FAT-equipped torpedoes were introduced late in 1942, and an early use was against convoy ONS-154 that December.

LUT *(Lagenunabhängiger Torpedo)*
This device was similar to the FAT, but produced a more irregular and variable course, and was not dependent on the initial angle of the firing boat to the

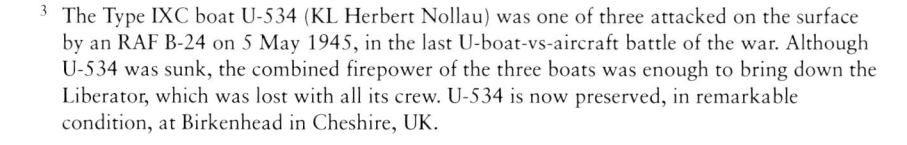

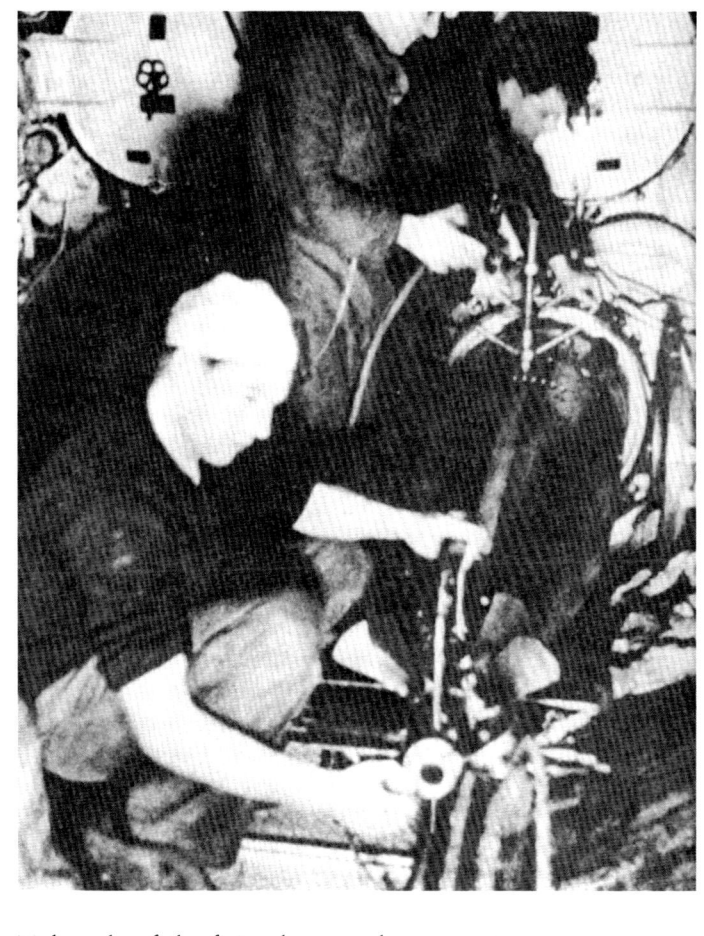

Final adjustments to the settings are made as a G7 torpedo is loaded into one of the lower bow tubes. (Author's collection)

---

[3] The Type IXC boat U-534 (KL Herbert Nollau) was one of three attacked on the surface by an RAF B-24 on 5 May 1945, in the last U-boat-vs-aircraft battle of the war. Although U-534 was sunk, the combined firepower of the three boats was enough to bring down the Liberator, which was lost with all its crew. U-534 is now preserved, in remarkable condition, at Birkenhead in Cheshire, UK.

F **THE *BACHSTELZE***

The unpowered *Bachstelze* gyrocopter **(inset 1)**, carried disassembled in containers on the rear Flak platform of a Type IX U-boat, could be launched like a kite at the end of a winch-cable when the boat was running into the wind at a good surface speed, and could carry an observer equipped with binoculars and a telephone link up to about 400 feet. This would multiply the U-boat's visual range from c.5 to c.25 miles, enabling the masts of shipping to be spotted when still well below the curvature of the earth from the viewpoint of the bridge watch **(inset 2)**. If the boat was forced to dive, the cable was cut and the pilot was left to his fate – although a parachute was fitted to the gyrocopter, in the faint hope that he could be found and picked up later. (The pilot would have to jettison the rotors by a quick-release device, otherwise he could not deploy the centrally mounted parachute.)

In fact only one merchantman is recorded as having been detected and subsequently destroyed thanks to the *Bachstelze*. On 5 August 1943, in the waters off Madagascar, the gyrocopter pilot of KK Robert Gysae's U-177 reported spotting the 4,195-ton SS *Efthalia Mari*, which was carrying about 4,800 tons of coal. Gysae began stalking her, and by early evening had manoeuvered U-177 into an ideal attack position. At 5.45pm he launched two torpedoes; the *Efthalia Mari* was fatally damaged, but sank slowly enough to allow her crew to take to the lifeboats. Another Type IXD-2 known to have used the *Bachstelze* was U-862; interestingly, it appears that the aerial observer on this boat was the medical orderly, Marineoberassiztenzarzt Jobst Schaefer. Although U-862 carried a gyrocopter on both her cruises to the Far East, there is no record of Schaefer successfully spotting any targets.

ABOVE
The purpose-built Type XB minelaying submarine was the largest class ever built, displacing over 2,700 tons fully loaded. The mines were carried in and discharged from vertical tubes spaced along the sides of the hull. (Deutsches U-Boot Museum)

BELOW
Overhead view of the hatches capping the mine tubes along the sides of the wide deck of a Type XB minelaying boat. (Deutsches U-Boot Museum)

target area. Unlike the FAT, which first followed a straight course before beginning its deviations, the LUT could effect a further change of course after firing and before going into its meandering pattern; the boat firing the torpedo could therefore be travelling parallel with the target convoy. The LUT-guided torpedo would first follow a straight course parallel with the convoy, then turn at right angles towards it and, on reaching the target area, begin its regular course changes. With LUT such course changes could be through more than 180 degrees, and the length of each 'leg' was infinitely variable between 0 and 1,500m, until its acoustic 'seeker' locked on to a target. LUT-equipped torpedoes were first used in 1944.

Mines

Germany possessed a number of specialized minelaying submarines such as the Type VIID and the Type XB. These were used for large-scale 'strategic' minelaying, and two such boats operating together could lay a fairly substantial mine barrage in a short time. The standard U-boat types could also carry mines as 'tactical' weapons, though in smaller numbers, launching either two or three (depending on type and dimensions) from each torpedo tube. Such small-scale minelaying was particularly useful in distant areas outside the range of minelaying aircraft, and in regions where Allied strength precluded the use of surface ships for this task.

The *U-Boat Commander's Handbook* instructs the commander to stand off an enemy port in darkness, making his preparations and laying course for the target area at first light. He was to observe the shipping channels, and to lay mines in the appropriate spots. Minelaying at night was not recommended due to the difficulty of accurate navigation in a blacked-out area where there was a danger of being taken by surprise, though it was accepted that minelaying on the surface at night could be successful for a sufficiently experienced commander. In fact, many of the U-boat 'aces' recorded significant numbers of the ships they sank being destroyed by mines rather than torpedoes. For example, in spring 1941 KL Jurgen Oesten was awarded the Knight's Cross for his success in sinking with mines eight ships, totalling nearly 45,000 tons, off the West African coast during his second patrol in U-106.

DEFENSIVE EQUIPMENT

Radar decoys: *Aphrodite*

Aphrodite consisted of a balloon stored in a canister on the submarine's deck. Once inflated with hydrogen it was approximately a metre in diameter, and it was anchored to a small raft or buoy by a line about 50m long. Suspended from the balloon were three strips of aluminium foil, to reflect radar pulses from the equipment carried on Allied aircraft or warships. Once launched, the balloon would stay aloft for approximately four to six hours, thus attracting the attention of the hunters while the U-boat slipped under the surface and escaped.

Thetis

This equipment, although theoretically effective, proved a total failure in service. It consisted of a small buoy carrying an assembly of steel tubes and sheets resembling a sail; as with Aphrodite, it was carried in disassembled form and initially had to be launched from the deck of a surfaced U-boat, though a more advanced form was developed that could be launched from the torpedo tubes. Like Aphrodite, its purpose was

This interesting shot shows the view down into the conning tower and then into the control room of a U-boat, as seen from the bridge; note the commander's white-topped cap at the bottom of the ladder. It is easy to visualize the difficulty of getting the entire bridge watch of at least five men – and often at least twice that many, on the later boats with heavier Flak armament – down through this little aperture, in the bare 25–30 seconds available during a crash-dive. (Author's collection)

to provide a radar signature resembling that of a surfaced submarine, and it was intended to sow large numbers around the Bay of Biscay, the 'Black Pit' through which U-boats had to run the gauntlet of Allied aircraft on their way to and from their bases on the Atlantic coast of France. As in the case of the 'Window' metal foil strips dropped by RAF night bombers, the idea was to confuse the enemy's radar by giving the impression of large numbers of targets among which the genuine ones would be indistinguishable. Unfortunately for the Germans, more advanced Allied radar sets did not pick up the reflections from these decoys, rendering the whole exercise pointless.

Sonar decoys: *Bolde* and *Sieglinde*

Also known as the *Pillenwerfer* ('bubble-thrower'), *Bolde* was a simple but effective device intended to deceive the Asdic on surface vessels hunting for U-boats. It was a tubular canister about 10cm in diameter, filled with calcium

G — SURFACE & UNDERWATER DETECTION

This diagram shows the typical effective range of the detection equipment used by both U-boats and Allied escort warships in spring 1943. The reach of the passive systems is shown as straight arrows, that of transmitted pulses as a series of arcs.

Sound travels great distances under water, and a U-boat **(U)** had passive hydrophones that could pick up the cavitation of ships' screws up to 100km (60 miles) away **(H)**, though they could not determine exact course or distance. Many Allied ground stations all around the Atlantic coasts were equipped with very long-range direction-finding interception radios, which could read and take a bearing from a strong signal source – certainly, from any transmission powerful enough to link U-boats in the Atlantic with BdU on the European mainland. Eventually, triangulation from several stations could place a U-boat within a 50-mile area of the ocean. From mid-1941 High Frequency Direction Finding ('huff-duff') sets, capable of fixing the briefest transmission, also began to be fitted in Allied warships; even following up a single bearing **(DF)** enabled an escort or support-group ship **(E1)** to get within the 40km (25 mile) range of her Type 272 search radar **(SR)**, which could then guide her closer to a surface target (again, a single set could read a bearing and rough distance, and more than one ship could triangulate a position more accurately).

Germany's delayed radar programme, and above all the unavoidably low position of any antennae mounted on a U-boat (as opposed to the mast-top antennae on Allied warships), were major handicaps. From around July 1942 boats began to receive the FuMB/Metox passive radar-pulse detection system, which could pick up Allied active radar from a maximum of 30km (18.6 miles) **(M)**. But Metox gave no accurate range; could not distinguish shipborne from airborne radar; could only be used on the surface, thus exposing the boat to the longer-ranged Allied radar; and was anyway distrusted by boat commanders – wrongly convinced that Allied ships could get a fix on the set, they often left it switched off. From late 1942 the first boats began to receive an active search radar of their own, FuMO 61 Hohentweil **(F)**; this was not as effective as Allied equipment, but in perfect conditions it could pick up a ship at 7km (4.3 miles).

Once an escort **(E2)** got within 2,000 yards of a U-boat, it could start hunting with its active Asdic **(A)**.

Inset 1: If two or more escorts were hunting together – as was very likely by this stage of the war – the U-boat's bearing and range could be triangulated for a depth-charge run by one of the warships, though before the introduction of improved Type 147 Asdic during 1943, escort captains had to rely on experience and instinct to guess the target's depth. A 'creeping' tactic was favoured in 1943 by the Royal Navy's greatest sub-killer, Cdr F.J. Walker of 2nd Escort Group. After his approach forced a U-boat into a deep dive, he sat on its tail to 'drive' it with clearly-audible Asdic 'pings'. At low speed to keep down propeller noise, a second escort circled ahead and waited in ambush; on Walker's signal, this then dropped 26 deep-set depth charges.

Inset 2: However, there was an Asdic 'blind spot' once the pursuer got within c.300 yards, when the 'ping' and its return echo became virtually simultaneous. If he had enough nerve to wait, an experienced U-boat commander could exploit this by making a hard turn. (Alternatively, it was not unknown for a commander to keep his boat in the 'shadow' directly below a slow-moving escort for some time.) During 1943–44 the 'blind spot' ahead of warships was steadily eliminated by the introduction of the Hedgehog multiple forward-firing mortar; at first difficult to operate, in 1944 – in concert with the new depth-finding Type 147 Asdic – this achieved an average kill-rate of one boat in every four attacks.

Inset 3: To counter last-minute turns, Walker adopted 'carpet-bombing' attacks. Again, the directing warship drove the U-boat ahead of it; but close on either beam, two other escorts kept station without 'pinging' – the cavitation noise of three ships moving at the same slow speed in close company on the same course could easily be mistaken for a single ship. They then all speeded up together and overtook the U-boat, dropping enough depth-charges to 'plaster' a wide enough area of sea to prevent any last-minute escape by course-changes. This tactic was first tried in June 1943 against U-202; after enduring 250 depth charges KL Günther Poser was forced to surface, and his boat was destroyed by gunfire. (Walker was relentless, and did not care how long he hunted or how much ordnance he expended. On a single patrol in February 1944, Capt Walker's 2nd Support Group sank six U-boats.)

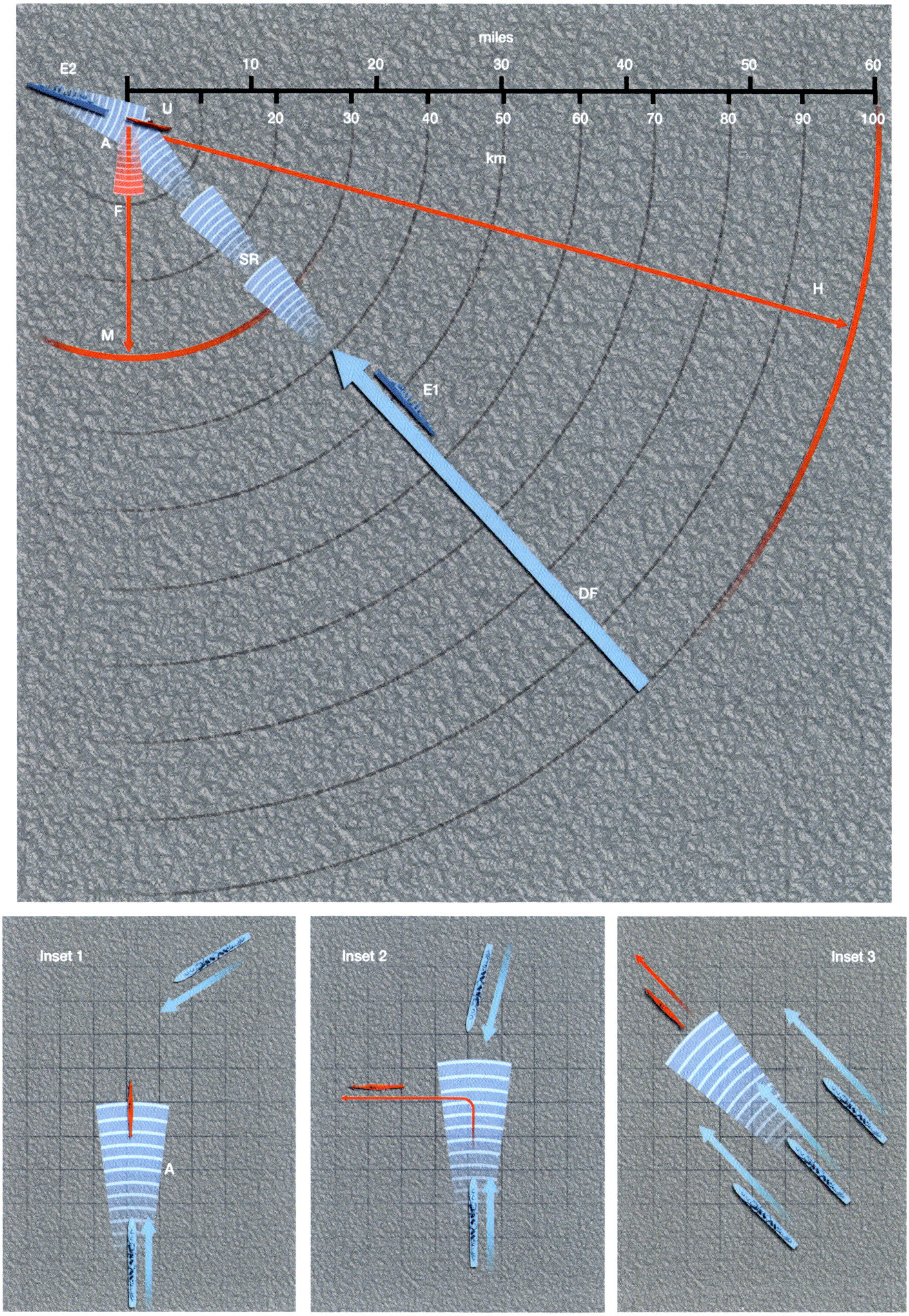
miles
10
20
30
40
50
60
E2
U
A
20
30
40
50
60
70
80
90
100
km
F
SR
H
M
E1
DF
Inset 1
A
Inset 2
Inset 3

RIGHT
One method of improving the rate at which a U-boat could dive was by narrowing the external hull just behind the bow, as seen here on U-190, a Type IXC boat; the weight of water flowing over this narrow waisted area increased the dive rate. Once an aircraft located a surfaced U-boat with its radar the aircrew usually turned the set off and tried to stalk the submarine under cover of clouds, breaking out for an attack run when only 40–50 seconds' flying time from the target. Every second shaved off the dive time could mean the difference between life and death. (Deutsches U-Boot Museum)

BELOW
A dramatic shot taken through the main navigation periscope, showing the bows of a Type IX boat broaching the surface as she rises from the deep. This is a good example of the field of view that could be seen through the periscope of a submarine. (Deutsches U-Boot Museum)

hydride; when it was ejected into the sea a valve allowed the ingress of water which reacted with the chemical, causing a large amount of gas to be emitted. The canister would remain at the same depth, the valve opening and closing and emitting gas bubbles for up to 20 minutes. To Asdic operators the sound signature of the mass of bubbles closely resembled that of a submerged submarine. While the escort gave its full attention to this false signal it was hoped that the U-boat could creep off, getting far enough from the warship to avoid detection by the time the chemical was exhausted.

The drawback was that once the U-boat started to move off the escort would be presented with two sonar signatures, one stationary and one moving, and would naturally go after the moving target. To get around this a new version called *Sieglinde* was given a tiny electric motor that propelled it through the water at around 6 knots, copying the Asdic signature of a moving U-boat far more realistically. This device was used in combination with Bolde, to increase the confusion of the sonar operators.

Siegmund

Rather than generating a false signal, this device was designed to detonate a sequence of several explosive charges to 'deafen' the Allied sonar equipment for a brief period. During the short spell following the first explosion the U-boat was supposed to put on a brief spurt of speed, then stop and await the next detonation, repeating the process until it had gained some distance from the attacker.

Alberich

Alberich consisted of coating-panels of a special synthetic rubber, to be attached to the entire outer skin of a submarine; this material reduced the detectable engine noise from the powerplant, and also the sound-echo reflected from the submarine by some 15 per cent. The patented material was a polyisobutene known as Oppanol; in the form used by the U-Bootwaffe it was made in 4mm-thick sheets, to be glued to the steel structure of the submarine. Initial tests on a Type II boat seemed promising, and it was decided to apply the coating to a new Type IXC, U-67, before she entered service.

Although the concept was sound (and is widely used today), the problem in 1941 was that a suitable adhesive had not been perfected. During U-67's short voyage to her first operational base with 2.Unterseebootsflotille at Lorient that August, it is estimated that at least 60 per cent of her Alberich coating was lost. Once the Alberich 'tiles' had loosened, the turbulence caused by the loose ends of partially detached panels flapping around in the current caused increased drag, and in fact a treated and 'peeling' submarine could end up more 'noisy' than an untreated one.

A suitable adhesive was only found in 1944, and when this was used to coat the Type VII boat U-480 with Alberich it was judged to be effective. On 25 August 1944, U-480 (Olt z S Hans-Joachim Förster) made an attack on convoy BTC-78 off the English coast near Lands End, sinking the freighter *Orminster*. By this late in the war very few boats would escape once detected by Allied surface ships, but although the escorts began a determined hunt they had to give up after seven hours, and the Alberich-treated U-boat escaped unscathed. Of course, it was not possible to determine to what degree her escape was due to the Alberich rather than simply to the skill of her

A rather apprehensive-looking crewman (centre) looks upwards as his shipmate tightens a valve. As a U-boat dived deep the increasing water pressure caused much creaking and groaning from the hull. This was naturally even more nerve-racking during depth-charge attacks, when alarming high-pressure leaks were not uncommon. (Deutsches U-Boot Museum)

ABOVE LEFT
The two crewmen operating the hydroplane controls on the forward starboard side of the control room. Their role was critical when the boat needed to crash-dive in an emergency. (Deutsches U-Boot Museum)

ABOVE RIGHT
The U-boat's cook or '*Smutje*'. This junior rating, provided with limited equipment, was responsible for keeping about 50 men well supplied with hot food and drink – a role so essential for morale that he was excused watch-keeping duty on the bridge. When a boat was manoeuvring defensively under absolute 'silent running' orders to escape Asdic-equipped hunters, and perhaps being shaken by depth-charge explosions, the cook's responsibility for keeping his pots and pans quiet was deadly serious. (Deutsches U-Boot Museum)

commander, but it was ordered that in future all new Type XXIII and Type XXVI boats should be treated with Alberich. In the event, only one Type XXIII, U-4709, had been treated before the war ended, and she was scuttled before undertaking any combat patrols.

Tarnmatte

A more successful attempt at improving stealth characteristics was the use of a synthetic rubber coating for the exposed head of the U-boat *schnorkel* or air intake/exhaust tube. The installation of this device was one of the German responses to the introduction in spring 1943 of Allied centimetric radar capable of detecting boats running on the surface day or night, which thereafter forced them to spend most of their time 'in the cellar'. This not only seriously degraded their ability to intercept Allied targets, but made the unavoidable periods spent running the diesel engines on the surface to recharge the electrical batteries extremely hazardous. The retractable *schnorkel* came into widespread use only in May 1944; it provided an air intake and exhaust for the diesels, so that boats could theoretically stay underwater 24 hours a day, not only charging batteries but cruising submerged (very slowly) on diesel power. However, not only was it difficult and even dangerous to operate, but its head above the surface could easily be detected by radar-equipped Allied aircraft.

The synthetic material used to coat the head was known as Buna; the thickness of the coating was dependent on the wavelength of the specific Allied radar emission, and to defeat the 9.7cm-wavelength ASV Mk III set the

54

Tarnmatte was applied 2cm thick. It was much more successful than Alberich, and was reported to be 90 per cent effective.

DEFENSIVE TACTICS

AGAINST WARSHIPS

Simply avoiding being seen was the priority for the U-boat commander, and both basic and more advanced 'stealth tactics' were used in hope of achieving this.

Simple colour schemes were important. To reduce the boat's visibility when seen against the light of the horizon, vertical surfaces above the waterline were generally painted pale grey; although some elaborate camouflage schemes were employed by individual boats, these were relatively rare. The horizontal surfaces (i.e. those that could be seen from above) were painted dark grey, making the boat more difficult to spot against the dark surface of the sea. Commanders were advised that 'all bright objects above decks, such as the insulators on the jump wires, should be painted in a dark colour. Paint which has washed off during operations must be replaced, and a supply of dark paint should be kept available for this purpose.' A U-boat running under the surface was very difficult to detect from the air unless the sea was very calm and the sun was shining very brightly, when the shadow of a shallow-running submarine might be visible.

U-boat commanders were constantly reminded that 'He who sees first has won', but had to balance the need to spot the enemy with the need to avoid

The bridge area and Flak platforms of an up-gunned Type VIIC boat, carrying a single-barrelled 3.7cm and two twin 2cm cannon. (Author's collection)

Note the heavy armour plates that have been installed around the upper part of the conning tower of this up-gunned Type VII boat, to give some measure of additional protection against fire from Allied aircraft. (Deutsches U-Boot Museum)

the enemy spotting them. Tips included the advice that the periscope should never be raised in daylight when lying on the surface, as it might reflect the sun, and was instantly recognizable as indicating the presence of a submarine. When diving, the periscope should not be raised until the boat was fully submerged; when surfacing, it should be fully retracted before the boat broached the surface. Commanders were advised, however, that if in a safe area, and any maintenance work required the periscope to be raised, it could be useful to have a lookout climb it, giving him a higher viewpoint and extending his range of vision.

Commanders were warned not to permit themselves to be seen on the horizon. If the mast of a potential enemy ship was spotted, they were advised to submerge no later than the moment when the top of the funnel came into view; warships might have lookouts posted up in the masts and might have rangefinders in the tops, and it was important to dive early enough to avoid being spotted. As the *U-Boat Commander's Handbook* warns, 'It is better to dive too soon, than too late – and [thus] to lose forever the chance to dive.'

Submariners were also advised that it might be preferable to remain submerged in poor visibility, such as fog, since at such times the boat's hydrophones would in any case pick up the sound of an approaching vessel before lookouts would be able to spot it – there was always the possibility of a boat running on the surface in fog being taken by surprise.

Commanders were warned to ensure that no oil leaks were leaving traces on the surface that might allow the boat to be tracked and detected; boats should also move away swiftly from the spot at which they submerged, in case patches of oil were left as the boat dived.

The official doctrine
Official recommendations for defensive manoeuvres were many and varied, including the following:

'If pursuit is long-lasting, the protection of darkness must be used wherever possible to escape on the surface.

'The most dangerous point is the moment at which the U-boat is spotted and begins its dive. At that point the enemy is aware of its location and direction of travel. The U-boat should therefore dive deep and leave the scene at full speed, not concerning itself at this point about the risk of sound detection.

'Once the enemy begins its hunt for the U-boat [using Asdic], all sources of noise in the boat should be minimized and all auxiliary machinery stopped. Rudder and hydroplanes should be operated by hand rather than by motor. The crew should speak only in low voices, work as silently as possible, and move around in stockinged feet.

'The U-boat should dive as deep as possible, since the greater the depth, the better the chance that the enemy will obtain incorrect Asdic readings.

'Do not make excessive use of zig-zagging, as this reduces the distance travelled from the enemy. Accelerate when the enemy accelerates, or when the detonation of depth charges conceals any additional engine noise. If the enemy stops, make only minimum revs to reduce engine noise. Always attempt to keep the stern pointing to the enemy in order to reduce the profile offered to the enemy Asdic.

'The U-boat which is under attack should always remain active, and not merely stop and passively wait in the hope that the enemy will fail to find it and depart.

'In certain circumstances, it can be acceptable to stop the boat and settle on the sea bed, especially at great depths where the Asdic will have difficulty locating the U-boat. This should only be a very temporary expedient, as leaks

This close-up view of a twin 2cm Flak cannon illustrates its large size; the padded arcs to the rear are shoulder-braces into which the gunner would lean when tracking his target. (Deutsches U-Boot Museum)

1

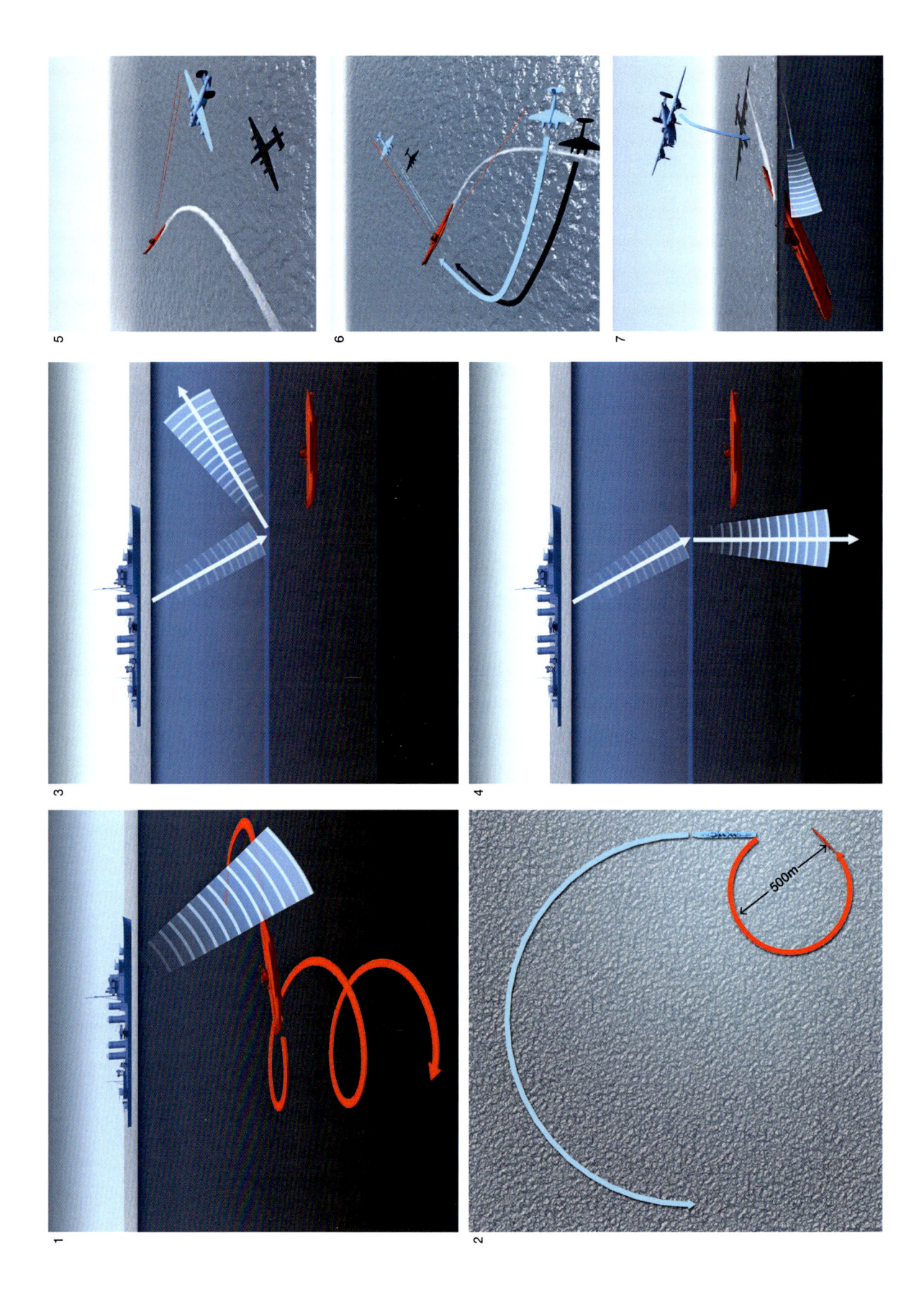

2

3

4

5

6

7

from e.g. oil storage tanks can rise to the surface and indicate the boat's position to the enemy. If attacked with depth charges, a close watch must be kept on all joints in case of leakage.

'The possibility of being forced to the surface must be considered, and preparations made for scuttling the boat, including placing demolition charges in locations such as the cooling water intake for the diesel engines, diesel exhaust pipes, and sea water inlet valves at the torpedo bulkheads. Charges must also be placed close to critical equipment such as wireless, sound location equipment, periscopes etc.

'Secret documents must be destroyed with acid if capture is imminent. Other documents should be weighted and jettisoned overboard.

'After surfacing for the last time, the diesel head and foot valves should be opened and the compressed air tanks blown. All available weapons should be used against the enemy to allow time for the destruction of the submarine and secret papers and equipment.'

* * *

U-boat commanders would use any or all of the above tactics to shake off an Allied warship. They were well aware of the limitations of Allied sound detection apparatus, and the U-boat's own passive hydrophones had a greater effective range than the active Asdic carried on the warships.

The U-boat could hear the Asdic 'ping' from its hunter long before the Asdic operator was able to pick up a return echo from the boat. When the warship got within about 300m the 'ping' and its echo became almost simultaneous, and thus useless for exact location, and the noise of the hunter's own screws as it ran in to attack at full speed drowned out the Asdic response; so at the last moment, instead of creeping away slowly and silently, the U-boat commander could risk increasing his own speed to maximum and manoeuvring to break free of the search pattern. Experienced submariners could also take advantage of the different thermal/salinity layers at various depths in the ocean, which could interfere with the Asdic signal. If a commander under depth-charge attack felt that he was pinned down, he

H: EVASIVE TACTICS
Escort vs U-boat

1: Once detected, the U-boat would make 'flank speed' while crash-diving, then apply full rudder and go into 'silent running' mode. The constant changes of direction as the boat spiralled into the depths would help confuse the pursuers' Asdic operators.

2: The U-boat might typically have a turning circle of some 500 metres. The old four-stacker destroyer shown here attacking it might have a turning circle two or three times greater than its quarry, and a submarine commander could exploit the tighter turns and generally greater manoeuvrability of his boat in many ways to evade his pursuers.

3 & 4: U-boats could also make use of thermal layers in the ocean, where changes in temperature and salinity could have the effect of deflecting Asdic pulses. **(3)** shows the pulse being refracted back towards the surface in winter seas. In **(4)**, the submarine hangs below a thermocline, where the temperature changes with depth at a greater rate than in the layers above or below, and the pulse is deflected straight to the bottom. Thermal layers did not make a submarine impossible to detect, just more difficult, and they were often found only at depths below the U-boat's safe diving limit.

Aircraft vs U-boat

5: When attacked, the U-boat would turn to keep its stern towards the aircraft; this offered as small a target as possible, while clearing the field of fire of its Flak guns. Long-range bombers like the B-24 had to carry maximum fuel, so only four to six depth charges; the chances of a straddling hit were improved by a run fore-and-aft at 50–100ft altitude, but this greatly increased the danger from Flak, and such aircraft had only light nose armament.

6: Faster Mosquitoes and Beaufighters had heavy forward-firing armament and could pick their own angles of attack, dividing the Flak fire and sweeping the conning tower area with a continuous burst of cannon fire and/or armour-piercing rockets.

7: In 1944 'Fido' air-dropped AS acoustic torpedoes reduced the risk to aircraft. Circling at a distance until the Flak crews went below for a crash-dive, they could then close from the stern and drop Fido in the U-boat's wake, to track its propellers.

Flak armament varied considerably from boat to boat; this one has single rather than twin 2cm guns on its upper platform, but the extremely effective quad-barrelled 2cm *Flakvierling* on the lower platform aft. The six 2cm barrels on this boat could throw up a devastating combined barrage of c.2,520 rounds of explosive and incendiary shells per minute. Although most engagements between aircraft and U-boats resulted in the destruction of the submarine, it is estimated that around 120 aircraft were shot down during attacks on U-boats, while about 30 of the hundreds of U-boats destroyed by aircraft went down fighting, attempting to defend themselves with their Flak armament. (Deutsches U-Boot Museum)

might resort to lying silently on the seabed and ejecting a small amount of oil and even some buoyant debris from a torpedo tube, in hope of giving the impression that his boat had already been destroyed.

AGAINST AIRCRAFT

From the outbreak of war Allied aircraft were potentially dangerous, though more of a nuisance than a dire threat; effective air-dropped depth charges and, above all, airborne search radar took time to develop. But their menace increased from mid-1941, with the introduction of CAM-ships – whose fighters could report a boat's position to warships, apart from strafing its bridge crew; and from spring 1943 convoys were often protected by escort carriers with Swordfish or Avenger AS attack aircraft. After the closing of the 'air gap' south of Iceland the constant risk of air attack increasingly preoccupied the U-boat commander's mind, both while crossing the Bay of Biscay and far out in the Atlantic. Even if nothing could be detected through the hydrophones, and a sweep with the periscope indicated that the ocean was clear all around the horizon, a surfacing boat could find itself under surprise attack from an aircraft slipping out of cloud cover at short notice. This was particularly nerve-wracking on a dark night, when centimetric radar could lead a bomber into position to turn on its 'Leigh Light' (see below) and make an attack run with less than a minute's warning. Recommended tactics for countering air threats included the following:

'1. In areas where there is a threat of attack by enemy aircraft, only the best members of the crew should be used on bridge watch, and anti-aircraft weapons should be manned and ready for action at all times. Weapons should be tested frequently to ensure that they are operational.

'2. U-boats should dive as soon as enemy aircraft are detected, unless the aircraft is not moving in the direction of the submarine. In this case the boat should avoid being spotted by turning away from the aircraft to offer the smallest profile, and slowing down to reduce the visible wake of the boat in the water.

'3. If an aircraft equipped with searchlights does not spot the U-boat until it flies directly over it, the boat should dive immediately, as it will take some time for the aircraft to turn and make another pass at the boat, giving time to escape.

'4. If the aircraft spots the U-boat from further away, the boat will not have time to dive safely, so should stay on the surface and use its anti-aircraft guns until the aircraft is directly overhead, then dive while the aircraft is turning to make its next attack run.'

It was sometimes possible for a U-boat to defend itself successfully with its Flak guns, and either escape or even shoot down its attacker, though that usually only happened when this was a lone patrol-bomber. On 1 March 1943, U-223 (KL Wachter) was caught on the surface by an RAF B-17 Flying Fortress. Taken by surprise and with no chance to dive, the U-boat was bombed with several depth charges and strafed by the air-gunners. However, the Flak crews remained at their stations, and their storm of fire caused significant damage to the Fortress's hydraulics and one of its engines. When the B-17 pilot turned to come in for a second pass only moments later he found that U-223 had taken the opportunity to crash-dive and had escaped, proving that a cool-headed commander could successfully implement Point 4 above.

While an engagement with an aircraft was not something any U-boat crew would wish to repeat, U-333 survived three such encounters. On 4 March 1943 a night-flying Wellington of RAF Coastal Command detected U-333 (Olt z S Werner Schwaff) on the surface with its radar, and caught the boat completely by surprise with its 'Leigh Light'; this powerful angled 24in searchlight mounted under the aircraft enabled the pilot both to locate the boat and to judge the correct range to drop depth charges. The boat's gunners were both quick and accurate, and managed to send the burning Wellington crashing into the sea. Of four depth charges it dropped, two missed the target, one bounced off, and another broke apart when it hit the casing and failed to detonate.

U-441, the first of the Type VIIs converted into true 'Flak boats'. Note both a 3.7cm gun and a 2cm *Flakvierling* mounted on the rear platforms, and a further quad gun platform is just visible forward of the tower; a 'bedstead' radar antenna is also visible above the bridge. U-441 was successful on her first mission, shooting down an RAF Sunderland flying boat on 24 May 1943. On her second mission, however, she drew the attention not of a lumbering Sunderland but of several fast, agile and heavily armed Beaufighters on 'Biscay patrol'. U-441 was badly battered; ten of her crew were killed and 13 wounded, including her commander KL Klaus Hartmann and all his officers. (Deutsches U-Boot Museum)

61

This was the scenario that every U-boat man setting out on operations hoped for – a safe return after a successful patrol, to be welcomed by their admired 'chief' Adm Karl Dönitz. In fact, of some 55,000 U-boat men who went to sea, about 27,490 never came home – a 50 per cent death rate, rivalled only by that in RAF Bomber Command. (Deutches U-Boot Museum)

On 11 June 1944, the lucky U-333 (now commanded by KL Peter 'Ali' Cremer) had already survived one aircraft attack that had damaged the boat so badly – including wrecking the 3.7cm Flak gun – that Cremer was returning to port. As the boat was limping home across the Bay of Biscay the following evening it was attacked yet again, by an RAF Sunderland. Even with its heavy AA gun out of action, U-333's 2cm gunners put up such a heavy and accurate barrage that the flying boat was shot down in flames.

The 'stand and fight' order

A typical Type VII boat of the early part of the war would carry only a single-barrelled 2cm Flak gun on its 'winter garden'. In 1943 the 8.8cm deck gun was often removed, and Flak capability was increased to one 3.7cm gun and two twin 2cm mounts on a double-terrace 'winter garden'; on some boats a quadruple 2cm *Flakvierling* mount was substituted for the 3.7cm gun, giving it a formidable defensive battery of up to eight 2cm automatic cannon.

The limitations of submerged speed and range meant that boats heading out or returning from patrol had to cross the Bay of Biscay on the surface. The advent of short-waveband radar and the Leigh Light increased the frequency with which such boats were surprised at night, prompting Dönitz to order a change of tactics at the end of April 1943. Now his boats were instructed to cross the Bay in daylight, submerging at night; the assumption was that in daylight the bridge watch would have a chance to spot aircraft at maximum range, gaining sufficient time to submerge – either before the aircraft could attack, or after delivering AA fire effective enough to at least buy the time to crash-dive. Unfortunately for the U-Bootwaffe, the RAF's Biscay patrols were strongly reinforced in early summer; and while the Allies could accept the average loss of one aircraft for one U-boat sunk, the Germans could not afford such arithmetic.

Aircraft could simply circle the U-boat while calling up air or surface reinforcements; the combination of a radar-equipped aircraft and an Asdic-equipped warship was the perfect anti-submarine team, while a boat attacked by more than one aircraft was forced to divide and therefore weaken its defensive fire. The 'stand and fight' order was rescinded at the end of July 1943, by which time it is reckoned to have cost 25 U-boats destroyed.

During June, Dönitz had ordered his boats to leave port in groups of about five, so that their combined Flak firepower could offer a greater degree of protection while crossing the Bay. The flaw in this was, of course, that if the attack persisted one boat would have to remain on the surface to deliver defensive fire while the others dived and, once alone, that boat might be doomed. This group self-defence tactic was not particularly successful. One occasion on which it worked was on 16 June 1944, when U-600, U-257 and U-615 successfully drove off an attack by RAF aircraft. On other occasions, however, outbound U-boats survived only at the cost of suffering enough damage to force them to return to base. On 11 June 1944 a group of five boats attacked by a Sunderland managed to shoot it down, but U-564 was sufficiently badly damaged to abort its mission; although U-185 also turned back to escort the damaged boat home, U-564 was sunk en route by a subsequent attack.

Flak boats

Dönitz's attempts to provide his boats with adequate AA defence culminated in the so-called 'Flak boats': a total of seven Type VIIC boats were to be converted by adding AA gun platforms fore and aft of the conning tower. However, the concept was fundamentally flawed: the additional weight raised the centre of gravity and destabilized the boat, and the additional drag reduced both speed underwater and operational range. The considerable additional manpower to operate the extra guns inevitably meant that it took longer to get everyone below deck when attempting to crash-dive. While the Flak boat's firepower was formidable, Allied aircraft might simply loiter out of range while waiting for warships to arrive in response to their sighting report. If the boat tried to dive in the meantime then the aircraft would be able to attack and sink it, since it was defenceless once committed to the dive. After an isolated success by U-441 in May 1943, the experiment was abandoned. One Flak boat, U-621, was sunk in action; the others whose conversion had been completed – U-441, U-256 and U-953 – were reconverted to conventional configuration, and work was cancelled on the last three.

SELECT BIBLIOGRAPHY

Edwards, Bernard, *Dönitz and the Wolfpacks* (Arms & Armour Press, 1996)
Franks, Norman & Zimmermann, Eric, *U-Boat vs Aircraft* (Grub Street, 1998)
Herzog, Bodo, *U-Boote im Einsatz* (Podzun-Verlag, 1971)
Ireland, Bernard, *Battle of the Atlantic* (Leo Cooper, 2003)
Mallmann Showell, Jak P., *Hitler's Navy* (Seaforth Publishing, 2009)
Mallmann Showell, Jak P., *U-Boats under the Swastika* (Ian Allan, 1973)
Mallmann Showell, Jak P., *U-Boat Commanders and Crews 1935–45* (Crowood Press, 1998)
Mallmann Showell, Jak P., *U-Boat Warfare – Evolution of the Wolfpack* (Ian Allan, 2002)
Miller, David, *U-Boats* (Chatham Publishing, 1999)
Oberkommando der Kriegsmarine, *U-Boot Kommandanten Handbuch* (Berlin, 1942)
Stern, Robert, *Battle beneath the Waves* (Arms & Armour Press, 1999)
Tarrant, V.E., *The U-Boat Offensive 1914–45* (US Naval Institute Press, 1989)

INDEX

References to illustrations are shown in **bold**. Plates are shown with page locators in brackets.

Admiral Scheer 40
Aenos 34
aircraft: attacks on U-boats 60; Avenger 60; B-17 Flying Fortress 6, 61; B-24 Liberator 6, 47, **H**(59); Beaufighter 37, **H**(59); 61; BV 222: 40; Fa 330 Bachstelze 40–42, **41**, **F**(47); Fw 200 Condor **B**(19), **37**, 38–39; He 111 and He 177: 40; Hurricane **38**, 39; Ju 88: 40; Mosquito 37, **H**(59); Sunderland 6, **61**, 62, 63; Swordfish 60; Wellington 42, 61; Wildcat 39; *see also* defensive tactics against aircraft
Alexia 8, 9
Archangelsk 42
Ark Royal, HMS 26, 27
'Asdic' (sonar) equipment 5, **G**(50), 52, 57, 59
attacks, convoy night surface *see* convoy night surface attacks
attacks, deck-gun *see* deck-gun attacks
attacks, 'wolf-pack' *see* 'wolf-pack' attacks
Audacity, HMS 39

Barham, HMS 25, 27
Baron Blythswood 9
Baron Pentland 36
Berury 36
binoculars: UZO equipment 8
Bletchley Park 4, 34
bridge, use of 7
bridge watch **2**, 7, 26, **E**(34), 39, **F**(47), **49**
Bülow, KK Otto von **2**
Bulysses 36

'CAM-ships' (Catapult Armed Merchantmen) **38**, 39, 60
Canadian Star 44
Catherine 19
Chambly, HMCS 36
chronology of U-boat war in Atlantic 6–7
Cleanthis 19
commanders, 'ace' 24
conning tower interior **49**
control rooms 25, 54
convoy formations **C**(22)
convoy interception by single U-boats **B**(19)
convoy night surface attacks 5–6, 8–10, **A**(10), 12–13; Kretschmer method, 1940–41 8–10, 12; official doctrine, 1943 12–13
convoys: BTC-78 37; HG-76 39; HX-72 9, 33–34; HX-112 7; HX-229 6, 44; MKS-30 40; OB-191 8–9; OG-69 39; OG-74 39; ONS-5 37; ONS-18 44–45; ONS-154 37; ONS-17 39–40; PQ-18 39; SC-7 10, 12, 34; SC-42 **E**(34), 36; SC-48 **E**(34); SL-139 40
cook 54
Cremer, KL Peter 'Ali' 62
Cyclops 28

deck-gun attacks **14**, 14–17, **17**, 19–21; official doctrine 20–21; the practice 16–17, 19–20; the theory: rules for interception of merchant ships 15–16, **17**
deck-gun firing crew **14**
decoys, Allied 'Foxer' 45
defensive equipment 49–50, 52–55; coating, *Alberich* 53–54; coating, *Tarmatte* 54–55; explosive charges, *Siegmund* 52; sonar decoys, *Bolde* 7, 50, 52; sonar decoys, *Sieglinde* 52; *see also* radar decoys
defensive tactics against aircraft **H**(59), 60–63; 'Flak boats' **61**, 63; 'stand and fight' order 62–63
defensive tactics against warships 55–57, 59–60; official doctrine 56–57, 59
detection, surface and underwater **G**(50)
Diggins, KL Kurt 5
diving 52, 53, 54
Dommes, KK Wilhelm 29
Dönitz, Grossadmiral Karl **4**, 19, 28, 29, 36, 37, 62, 62, 63
Dresky, KL Hans-Wilhelm von 17

Eck, KL Heinz-Wilhelm 42
Efthalia Mari, SS 41, 42, **F**(47)
Elin K. 44
Elmbank 9
Empire Crossbill 36
Empire Hudson 36
Empire Whimbrel 19
Empress of Britain 37
engine room 4
engineering officer and crew 13
'Enigma' automatic encryption machines 4, 6, 34
equipment 40–43; *Bachstelze* gyrocopters 40–42,

41, **F**(47); *Biber*-type midget-submarines 42–43 *see also* defensive equipment
Escort Group B7 37
Everett, Lt 39

Far Eastern waters, 1943–44: solo missions 29, 32
First Watch Officer 8
'Flak boats' **61**, 63
Flak platforms **41**, 55
Förster, KK Hugo 36
Förster, Olt z S Hans-Joachim 53

Garm 36
Göring, Reichsmarschall Hermann 37
Greger, Olt z S Eberhard **E**(34)
'group' tactics 29
Gruppen: 'Amsel' 37; 'Fink' 37; 'Markgraf' **E**(34); 'Monsoon' 29; 'Mordbrenner' **E**(34); 'Preussen' 37; 'Star' 37
Guggenberger, KL Friedrich 26, 27
gunnery practice **14**
Gypsum Queen 36
Gysae, KK Robert 41, **F**(47)

'Happy Time' 34; 'Happy Time, Second' 6, 28
Hardegen, KL Reinhard 28
Hartmann, KL Klaus 61
HFDF (High Frequency Direction Finding) **G**(50)

Invershannon 9
Itchen, HMS 44–45

James Oglethorpe 44
Jedmore 36

Kretschmer, KK Otto 5, 8, 9, 9–10, 12, 16–17, 34; night surface attack method, 1940–41 8–10, 12

Langan, HMS 44
Languedoc 34
Leberecht Maas 37–38
Leitender Ingineur (engineering officer) 13
Leticia 17
lookouts 7, **26** *see also* bridge watch
Lucerna 8
Luftwaffe: KG 26: 40; KG 30: 40; I/KG 40: 37, 38; 3/KG 40: 39
Luftwaffe/Kriegsmarine co-operation 37, 37–40; combined air-sea strikes 39–40; Fw 200C Condor 38–39
Luimneach 17
Lüth, KK Wolfgang 19
Lützow 40

Malaya, HMS 26, 27
Maplin, HMS 39
Max Schultz 37–38
Mediterranean solo missions 26–27
Merisaar 16–17
Moose Jaw, HMCS 36
Muneric 36

navigation 32, 33
night surface attacks, convoy *see* convoy night surface attacks
Nollau, KL Herbert 47
North American waters, 1942: solo missions 27–29
North Atlantic conditions **31**, 39
Norwegian campaign (1940) 14

Obermaschinist (technical senior petty officer) 13
Obersteuermann (coxswain) 32, 33
Oesten, KL Jürgen 48
Olivegrove, SS 17
Operation: 'Drumbeat' 28; 'Torch' 36–37
Orminster 17

periscopes: 'attack' 36; navigation ('sky') 5, 52
planesmen 25, 54
Polyanthus, HMS 44
Poser, KL Günther **G**(50)
Prien, KL Günther 9, 17, 19, **22**, 24, 25, 26, 34
Prize Ordinance Regulations (1936) 15

'Q-ships' 15
Queen Elizabeth, HMS 27

radar: ASV Mk III centimetric 54–55; Type 272 search **G**(50)
radar decoys 49–50; *Aphrodite* 7, 49; *Thetis* 49–50
Reche, KL Reinhard 40
refuelling 28
Reschke, KL Franz-Georg 27
return from patrol **62**
Royal Air Force 62; Coastal Command 61
Royal Navy: Force H 26

Royal Oak, HMS **22**, 25, 26
rules of engagement 15, 20

Sally Maersk 36
Scania 36
Scapa Flow **22**, 22, 25–26
Schafer, Marineoberassiztenzarzt Jobst **F**(47)
Schepke, KL Joachim 34
schnorkel (air intake/exhaust tube) 54
Schwaff, Olt z S Werner 61
Scoresby 34
searchlights, 'Leigh Light' 37, 60, 61, 62
Sicilia 19
solo missions 21–22, **24**, 24–29; *Einzelstellung* type 21–22; Far Eastern waters, 1943–44 29, 32; *Freijagd* type 22, 28; *Lauerstellung* 22; the Mediterranean: U-81 and U-331 26–27; North American waters, 1942 27–29; U-47 at Scapa Flow 25–26
Spahr, KL Wilhelm 29
St. Croix, HMS 44
Stargard 36
Steinhoff, KL Friedrich 41
Stonepool 36
stores, loading **27**
Strinda 8
surface approaches, optimum **A**(10); *see also* convoy night surface attacks

Tahchee 36
Thistleglen 36
Tiesenhausen, KL Hans-Diederich Freiherr von 25, 27
Tirpitz 40
Topp, KL Erich 5
torpedo aiming system: UZO equipment 8
torpedo guidance systems: FAT **E**(34), 47, 48; LUT **E**(34), 47, 48
torpedo tubes, loading 44, 45, 47
torpedoes 5–6, 43–45, 47–48; fanned salvos 10; G7 14, **43**, **F**(47); G7e *Falke* acoustic **43**, 43, 44; G7e T5 *Zaunkönig* 44–45; G7e T10 *Spinne* 45; G7e T11 45, 47
Trevisa 34

U-Boat Commander's Handbook 10, 12–13, 17, 20–21, 49, 56
U-boat types: Type VII 5, **14**, 21, 28, 39, 42, 43, 43, 44, 56, 62; Type VIIC **2**, 20, 28, 55, 61, 63; Type VIID 48; Type IX **15**, 16, 28, 29, 41, 44, **F**(47), 52; Type IXC 52; Type IXD 41; Type IXD-2 'monsoon' 29, 41, 52, 28–29; Type XB **48**, 48; Type XIV Tanker-cargo (*Milch-Kuhe*) 28; Type XXIII 54; Type XXVI 54
U-boats: U-32 33, 34; U-33 17; U-38 34; U-46 34; U-47 9, 17, 19, **22**, 22, 25–26, 33, 34; U-48 33, 34, 43; U-57 6; U-66 28; U-67 33; U-68 39; U-79 39; U-81 26, 27, 36; U-82 36; U-85 **E**(34); U-90 32; U-98 36; U-99 8–9, 10, 12, 16–17, 33, 34; U-100 33, 34; U-101 33; U-106 48; U-109 28; U-123 28, 34; U-124 34; U-125 28; U-126 39; U-130 28; U-177 41–42, **F**(47); U-178 29; U-181 19; U-185 47; U-202 **G**(50); U-203 39; U-205 27; U-207 36; U-221 44; U-223 61; U-255 39–40; U-256 63; U-257 63; U-270 44; U-295 62; U-331 25, 27; U-333 61–62; U-338 44; U-377 45; U-404 2; U-432 36; U-441 61, 63; U-458 5; U-480 53; U-488 28; U-501 36; U-502 28; U-534 45, 47; U-561 39; U-564 63; U-600 63; U-603 44; U-615 63; U-621 36; U-652 36; U-666 44–45; U-716 42; U-758 44; U-852 36; U-862 **F**(47); U-873 41; U-952 44; U-953 63; U-954 47; U-972 45; U-992 42; U-4709 54
U-Flotille, 6.: **2**; U-Flotille, 7.: **22**
'Ultra' intelligence 4, 37
UZO (U-Boot Zieloptik) equipment 8

Valiant, HMS 25, 27

Wachter, KL 61
Walker, Cdr F.J. **G**(50)
Walker, HMS 12
Walter Q. Gresham 44
weapons, Allied: 'Fido' air-dropped AS acoustic **H**(59); mortar, Hedgehog **G**(50)
weapons, German: deck guns, 8.8cm 21, 39; deck guns, 10.5cm 19, 21; Flak cannon, 2cm 20, 21, 55, 57, 60, 61, 62; Flak gun, 3.7cm 21, 55, 61, 62; machine guns, 7.92mm 20; mines 48, 48–49; Type IX boats 16; *see also* torpedoes
Wintersvijk 36
'wolf-pack' attacks 29, 32–34, **E**(34), 36–37; fast patrol lines 36; patrol/reporting lines **D**(31), 32–34, **E**(34); turn of the tide 36–37

Zaanland 44

64